KEEP COO
–The Maine Way

More
Favorite
Down East Recipes
By
Marjorie Standish

Author *of*
COOKING DOWN EAST

Sketches by Edward A. Materson

Down East Books
Camden, Maine

ISBN 0-89272-391-2

5

Down East Books
P.O. Box 679
Camden, ME 04843

TO GEORGE

THE MAN IN MY LIFE

About the Author

Start talking about cooking Down East — that is, the Maine way — and chances are the name Marjorie Standish won't be long in entering the discussion.

Twenty-five years of collecting, testing and sharing Maine recipes through her Maine Sunday Telegram column, "Cooking Down East," brought her statewide recognition and acclaim. And in 1968 her first cookbook, of that name, was published in response to requests of many readers for a handy compilation of favorite recipes, which have since found their way into kitchens of relatives and friends throughout Maine and most other states.

Marjorie Holbrook (later Mrs. George A. Standish) received a B.S. degree in home economics from Farmington Normal School in 1931. She taught that subject in Maine high schools before joining the Central Maine Power Company as home service advisor and later becoming its home service coordinator.

In 1969 Mrs. Standish won the Woman-of-the-Year Award granted by the Maine Press, Radio and TV Women. In 1973 she was the recipient of an Award of Appreciation from the Maine Department of Agriculture. And the University of Maine at Farmington honored her at its 1973 Commencement by awarding her the college's first Distinguished Service Award.

Mrs. Standish and her husband moved to Augusta in 1966 after residing in Gardiner 29 years. Both retired in 1973.

FOREWORD

Not everyone gets a chance to write a second cookbook. That's the reason I feel so grateful that this book came about. After the success of "Cooking Down East," I guess another book sort of became inevitable.

One of the main reasons it seemed justified was the recollection of how hard it had been to select the recipes for "Cooking Down East" when so many favorites were available. Many readers of my Maine Sunday Telegram column had urged me to write a book and be sure to include their favorites.

Space limitations made it impossible to include them all. And since then, dozens and dozens more have appeared in the column to add new favorites to the list. For those who like my first book and want more of the same, this book is the answer.

You know, we all have a special way of telling the Maine story. Happily, for 25 years my way has been through writing the "Cooking Down East" column in the Sunday Telegram.

Actually, it dates back longer than that for me. Like growing up down on the New Meadows River and learning at an early age what Down East cooking is all about.

Maine cooking is a way of life. It is evident as you use these recipes. You will find all kinds; they came from our family and they came from yours. If you felt proud enough of your family recipes to share them in my column, then they have deep meaning for all of us. They are cherished recipes.

Some of these recipes are old, making us aware that our forebears made do with what was at hand. They have been up-dated so amounts are definite and directions are clear, for that is the way we like to cook.

You will find your favorite contemporary recipes, too. They will have significance for you as they do for me, and you will agree they represent life in the Pine Tree State.

It is like opening a treasure chest to share a recipe. In Maine, we like to build our recipes around foods for which we are noted. We enjoy using recipes that show off our Maine food products to their best advantage. We like to think that as Maine cooks so do a lot of other people in the country, for this exchange of recipes is far-reaching.

Amazing as it seems, we still cook "from scratch," for it is our heritage. Of course, we like the convenience foods and all the short cuts. They are not exactly new to us; think of all the years we've been opening a can of soup. Now there are new and exciting ways we can produce a meal quickly when time is short.

Hopefully, this cook's tour I am taking you on that combines the old with the new will furnish you with reading and recipes to keep you cooking—the Maine way.

September, 1973

TABLE OF CONTENTS

Soups
Stews
&
Chowders

Too many cooks spoil the broth

CHAPTER ONE

Soups, Stews and Chowders

Maine is soup and chowder country. From the days of the heavy black soup kettle, with its contents simmering on the back of the old black cookstove, to the cutting edge of Now, we're for soups, stews and chowders.

There are quick and amazing ways to make soups, and we like the availability of these methods. Yet Maine cooks think in terms of longer cooking periods when they have a soup or stew in mind. There is an economical stability about these old recipes and the richness and nutritional value cannot be overlooked.

A Maine housewife has various ways of using an extremely low heat to do long, slow cooking. She remembers hearing her grandmother tell about the fireless cooker she learned to make in Farm Bureau years ago for this kind of cooking. Even now, you are apt to find one tucked away under the eaves in an old farmhouse attic.

Her mother talked of the deep-well cooker of her electric range, where she could cook stews or soups overnight or all day at very low cost. Kitchens became more streamlined, ranges were built to fit. The deep-well cooker had to go.

Today's Maine housewife has a simmering heat available on her kitchen range. Or she is apt to have a deep cooker on her kitchen counter, a separate appliance where again she turns to all-day or all-night cooking with the lowest cost of operation she could wish.

This is our way of life, and with great pride we call up from the past and present old standbys and simple up-to-date recipes to whet the appetites of all ages in the future.

★Pea Soup was always served with johnnycake, and still is. After all, when you combine the economy of this rich, wholesome soup with the solid comfort of johnnycake, you've got a real meal going.

OLD-FASHIONED SPLIT PEA SOUP

1 pound dried split peas, yellow or green	1 potato
1 onion	Salt
1 carrot	Pepper
	2 quarts water

Wash peas and put in kettle; cut and add vegetables. Add seasonings and water. If ham stock is available, use some of that and 3 tablespoons of fat; otherwise, use a ham bone or smoked pork chop or ¼ pound salt pork. Cover kettle, bring to steaming point, lower heat and cook slowly for about 3 to 4 hours. Stir occasionally, to prevent scorching. Remove meat and fat. Strain soup, pressing vegetables through sieve, or use a food mill. Cut any bits of ham or smoked pork chop if used and add to soup. Add 1 cup cold milk and reheat. Serves 6.

★Cornbread was made by the Indians before us, as everyone knows. Whether you call it cornbread or johnnycake (which I cling to), it was once upon a time called journeycake. No matter what you call it, this recipe for Spider Johnnycake is right to serve with Pea Soup. In Maine, when we refer to a spider, we mean a cast-iron pan with a handle, used for frying. Originally with legs, it was used over coals on the hearth. If you do not own a spider, then use an 8 x 8-inch pan for baking this johnnycake.

SPIDER JOHNNYCAKE

¾ cup cornmeal	1½ cups, plus 2 tablespoons milk
¼ cup sifted flour	
1 tablespoon sugar	1 egg, well beaten
½ teaspoon salt	2 tablespoons margarine
1 teaspoon baking powder	

Sift dry ingredients. Add 1 cup plus 2 tablespoons of the milk and beaten egg. Mix only to dampen dry ingredients. Melt margarine in frypan or 8 x 8-inch pan. Turn mixture into pan, pour remaining ½ cup milk over batter. Do not stir. Bake at 400 degrees for 25 to 30 minutes. Serve piping hot. Serves 4.

CREAM OF TOMATO SOUP

4 tablespoons butter or
  margarine
3 tablespoons flour
2 teaspoons salt
A bit of black pepper
2 cups milk

2½ cups canned tomatoes
1 tablespoon minced onion
¼ teaspoon celery seed
½ teaspoon sugar
½ bay leaf
1 whole clove
⅛ teaspoon baking soda

Melt butter or margarine in a double boiler, then add flour, 1½ teaspoon salt and the pepper. Blend. Add milk; stir until thickened. Meanwhile cook together the tomatoes, onion, celery seed, remaining ½ teaspoon salt, sugar, bay leaf and clove for 5 minutes. Strain, add soda, then add to thickened milk mixture gradually, while stirring constantly. Heat 1 minute, continuing to stir. Serves 4 to 6.

★You will want to refresh your memory with this recipe for Tomato Bisque. It's strictly Maine-ish. You will recall your mother used to make it and it will be good to acquaint your own family with this easy-to-make soup.

TOMATO BISQUE

2 cups canned tomatoes
4 cups milk
4 tablespoons butter
  or margarine

Pepper
Salt
1 teaspoon sugar

Put tomatoes in a saucepan, juice too, chop tomatoes into small pieces. Add the butter, sugar, pepper and salt, bring to a boil. Boil about 5 minutes. Add milk and bring again to a boil. Serve as is, without straining. Don't ask me why it doesn't curdle, but it doesn't. Serves 6.

★Making-do has been the slogan of Maine cooks as far back as anyone can remember. It could be the reason sturdy Maine vegetables have been used as the basic ingredient in many soup recipes. Baked Bean Soup for instance. There is every reason for using left-over baked beans when the soup is so delicious. Or Parsnip Stew, which really isn't a stew at all; more like a chowder. If you have never made it, you should and learn why our forebears decided it was a cherished way of using parsnips. Best of all, Cream of Potato Soup was yet another way of producing a hearty soup from Maine's best known vegetable.

BAKED BEAN SOUP

2 cups leftover baked
  beans, juice and all
2 cups water
1 large onion, peeled
  and quartered

2 cups canned tomatoes,
  undrained
1 tablespoon butter
Salt and pepper
  to taste

Put beans, onion and water into kettle and simmer slowly for 1 hour. Remove from heat and rub all through a sieve or use a food mill. Return to kettle, add tomatoes to bean mixture, and simmer 1 hour longer. Season to taste with salt and pepper and add butter. Serves 4. This is good reheated.

★You will find parsnips in our markets almost year round. I like them best when a neighbor or friend lets them stay in his garden all winter, then digs them to share as a very special part of springtime in Maine. They're almost as good as dandelion or fiddlehead greens. Keep in mind that parsnips have a sweet flavor.

PARSNIP STEW

2 slices salt pork (or use
  2 tablespoons margarine)
1 small onion, diced
2 cups diced potatoes
2 cups water

Salt and pepper to taste
3 cups parsnips, cut
  in cubes
1 quart milk
4 tablespoons margarine

We say, "try out" salt pork. It means to cook slowly, using a low heat. Remove pieces of pork, add onion and cook gently. You may favor using margarine; in that case cook onion in it. Add diced potatoes, water, salt and pepper; cover kettle, bring to steaming point. Cook potatoes 10 minutes, then add cubed parsnips which do not take as long to cook. Return cover and cook for 10 minutes, after steaming point is again reached. Test for doneness and add milk. Season to taste. Add margarine or butter, if it has not been used in place of salt pork. Some cooks like to add ½ cup rolled out cracker crumbs for thickening. Serve bowls of Parsnip Stew topped with minced parsley. This recipe serves 6.

CREAM OF POTATO SOUP

2 cups small diced, pared, raw potatoes
2 minced medium onions
2 stalks celery, including leaves, diced
2½ cups boiling water
4 tablespoons butter or margarine

3½ tablespoons flour
1½ teaspoons salt
¼ teaspoon black pepper
2 cups milk
1 tablespoon minced parsley

Cook potatoes, onions, celery in the boiling water, covered, until very tender. Meanwhile melt the butter in top double boiler. Add flour, stir until smooth; then add seasonings and milk. Cook while stirring until smooth and thickened. Then rub the potato mixture, liquid and all, through a sieve. You should have 3 cups puree. Add to sauce with parsley; heat and serve. Serves 6.

★In Maine we like Beef Stew and we enjoy serving it for company. There is a sturdiness about it that makes it very filling. There are such attractive Dutch ovens that may be brought to the table for serving, you may decide to try this Oven Beef Stew. If you are using your oven anyway, then this covered pan of stew may simmer away in a corner of the oven and not be any trouble.

OVEN BEEF STEW

2 pounds stew beef
2 tablespoons margarine
  or salt pork fat
Flour to dredge beef
1 tablespoon salt
¼ teaspoon pepper
4 cups hot water
¼ cup catsup

1 bay leaf
2 large onions, peeled
  and quartered or sliced
6 carrots, pared and
  quartered
4 medium potatoes, pared
  and quartered
1 cup diced celery

Cut beef into 1-inch cubes. Put flour, salt and pepper into a paper bag, shake up beef in bag. Melt fat in heavy pan with tight fitting cover. This beef stew may be cooked on top of stove if you wish, but when done in the oven, it takes on almost a different flavor. Brown beef in melted fat. Add sliced onions, celery, catsup, bay leaf and hot water. Cover pan and place in 300-degree oven for 2½ hours. Add carrots and potatoes, replace cover, continue in oven at 300 degrees for 1 to 1½ hours longer, making certain the vegetables are tender.

Mix about 1/3 cup flour with 2/3 cup cold water, allow to set; then when Oven Beef Stew is ready, add flour mixture to thicken. Return to oven, cover off, to be sure flour is cooked. Serve in soup dishes or bowls. Serves 6, generously.

LAMB STEW

2 pounds boned lamb
  shoulder
¼ cup flour
2 teaspoons salt
¼ teaspoon pepper
3 tablespoons margarine
1½ quarts boiling water
1 peeled clove garlic
3 medium carrots, pared
  and quartered

2 medium onions, peeled
  and quartered
3 pared large potatoes,
  quartered
1 medium turnip, pared
  and sliced
½ cup diced celery
¼ cup chopped parsley
1 teaspoon bottled thick
  condiment sauce

Remove any fat and gristle from lamb, cut meat into 1-inch cubes. Place flour, 1 teaspoon of salt, and pepper into paper bag; shake lamb cubes in this. Brown meat in melted margarine in a Dutch oven or deep kettle until well browned. Add boiling water and garlic, cover and simmer for 30 minutes.

Then add the carrots, onions, potatoes, turnips, celery, remaining teaspoon salt, some more pepper, and simmer, covered, for 1 to 1½ hours longer or until meat and vegetables are tender. Remove meat and vegetables to a hot platter and keep hot. Add condiment sauce to liquid left in Dutch oven or kettle. Thicken with a flour paste of 1/3 cup flour mixed with 2/3 cup water. Pour over meat and vegetables. Sprinkle parsley over all. Serves 6.

★It happened when Horace Hildreth was Governor of Maine. Maine cooks were asked to submit their favorite seafood recipes. The response was heartwarming. I was one of the judges for that contest. It was the sort of happening one could never forget. This Crabmeat Stew was a winner then and it still is.

CRABMEAT STEW

2 tablespoons butter
6 small soda crackers
2 cups fresh crabmeat
½ cup water

1 quart milk
Salt and pepper
1 tall can evaporated
  milk

Melt butter slowly in kettle. Roll crackers until crumbs are as fine as flour. Place these crumbs and the crabmeat in butter, add water, and let mixture bubble for one minute to bring out the luscious flavor of the crabmeat. Pour in the milk and stir until it is very hot, but do not boil. Add seasonings and evaporated milk. Reheat, but again do not boil. Serves 6.

★I've had my fair share of judging recipe contests and am very grateful for the opportunity. Not so many years ago, the Maine Dairy Council sponsored Maine Grange Dairy suppers during June — Dairy Month. I recall that the first time that we did it, 153 Maine granges entered this contest. Huntoon Hill Grange of Wiscasset won that first contest.

Their main dish which was strictly Maine was for Lobster Chowder. It was the first time I had known of lobster being used in a chowder.

LOBSTER CHOWDER

6 to 8 tablespoons butter
2 small onions, minced
4 medium sized potatoes, diced
Salt and pepper to taste

4 medium sized lobsters, or when cooked and picked out, enough to make 1 pound lobster meat
2 quarts milk, warmed

Cook the onion and potato in one cup water in a covered pan until they are tender. Add cooked lobster meat that has been cut into smallish pieces. Add butter. Stir with a fork to mix together and cook about 3 minutes. Warm the milk, then add to the lobster mixture. Season to taste. Allow to mellow. Serves 6 to 8.

SEAFOOD CHOWDER

2 slices salt pork
1 small onion, diced
2 cups water or bottled clam juice
3 cups pared and diced potatoes
1 pound haddock fillets
Salt and pepper
½ pound scallops

1 pint chopped clams, or 2 cans minced clams
1 can crabmeat or
2 cups fresh lobster meat or
2 cups Maine shrimp
2 quarts milk, scalded
1 stick butter or margarine

Fry out salt pork in kettle, remove pork scraps and cook diced onion in fat, gently. Add water or clam juice, potatoes, cover and cook about 15 minutes. Lay haddock fillets and fresh scallops on top of potatoes, simmer slowly just until fish "flakes" and scallops are done. It is best to quarter the scallops before placing them in kettle. If clams are uncooked, then they go into kettle at same time. If canned clams are used, then they are added with crabmeat, cooked lobster meat and cooked shrimp. Add scalded milk, stick of butter or margarine. Taste for seasoning. This chowder will be enough for 8 to 10 people.

Once the chowder is assembled, the top of double boiler is excellent for keeping until serving time and leaves far less chance of any curdling or "separation." This holds for any stew or chowder where milk is involved.

★Easy Maine Style Clam Chowder is easily prepared from ingredients you have stored in your cupboard. It has a delicious flavor and you will exclaim, "This is second best to a chowder made with fresh Maine clams."

MAINE STYLE
CLAM CHOWDER

3 slices salt pork
1 small onion, diced
One 8-ounce bottle clam juice
3 cups diced raw potatoes
Black pepper to taste

Two 8-ounce cans minced clams or whole clams
3 cups milk or one 14½-ounce can evaporated milk, plus 1 can water
Salt to taste
½ stick butter or margarine

Using a deep saucepan, fry salt pork slowly, remove and add diced onion. Cook on low heat until onion is soft. Add clam juice, diced raw potato and enough black pepper to satisfy your taste. Cover pan, bring to steaming point. Lower heat and cook at least 15 minutes.

Remove cover, add minced clams including juice, stir to mix. Cook about 10 minutes with cover off, allowing clams to simmer along in cooked potato mixture. Add milk, butter or margarine, heat to serving point. Taste for seasoning, add salt and more pepper as needed. Serves 4 to 6. If you wish, cut pieces of lightly browned salt pork into small bits and sprinkle on top of bowls of chowder before serving.

Fish and Shellfish

*"When one is hungry, frescoed walls
Can't take the place of codfish balls"*

CHAPTER TWO

Fish and Shellfish

"New Meadows flows the same today, with dancing
waters to the sea,
And tells its story all the way replete
with love and melody".

Moses Owen

Looking back, I like to think I grew up at a very good time. Of course a lot of people feel that way. My reason is that I remember the tiny community of New Meadows when it was at its best. The farms were large, the hayfields stretched in all directions, the vegetable gardens were big, there were woods roads to tramp, and probably I remember the pastures best of all.

Everyone kept cows, the number depending upon whether the farmer sold cream at Bath, only a few miles distant, or made butter to take to the grocery stores in Brunswick. I recall our pasture the best. There were grassy covered quarries in back of our barn and carriage house. Lime had been quarried and burned here years before by my Coombs ancestors. Our farm was on what was known as Limekiln Hill.

And then there was the beautiful New Meadows River, where our mother and father took my sister Doris and me swimming in special little coves, when the tide was in. After all, when the tide is out there is only a channel. I have always liked to talk about growing up on the New Meadows clam flats, a fact of which I am proud. I even liked the way they smelled.

Sometimes, Mother took Doris and me swimming in the creek. That was nearer the farm and we only needed to go to an upstairs window to see how the tide was coming into the creek.

The creek was where Harve Jordan, our next door neighbor, set his eel traps in the fall. I remember one fall when he converted a long hen house into the place where the eels were cleaned and readied for shipping to the New York market.

Summertime was very exciting, for so many peddlers called house to house in the farming areas. The day Mr. Alexander with his Grand Union Tea Co. wagon called was usually the best. Yet, there was the fruit peddler and the rag peddler, for everyone kept a ragbag. He was glad to pay you a few cents for your rags.

Just as exciting was the fish peddler, for his fish was extremely fresh. Once we had one who called and, for some unknown reason, he also sold fig jam. Most farms had a small ice house, so there was never too much of a problem about keeping food. The cellars with earthern floors were cool spots, too. In some farm homes they were the only way of keeping food cool in the summertime.

Dad had special flats where he dug our clams. I don't think he told others where they were. Back then, the New Meadows River banks were not lined with cottages as they are today. At our slightest wish he would get a clambake ready for us.

He fished for cunners off the rocks at Bailey Island. He would go to Cundy's Harbor to go Outside, deepsea fishing. It was a welcome sight when the Model-T turned into the yard on a late Sunday afternoon. I never did like those deepsea fishing trips too much.

Then came the task of drying and salting the fish. On a clear, cool summer's day he would have the salted fish out on the woodshed roof, drying in the sun. For a wintertime treat in the evening, we liked to go to the cellarway where a dried fish would be hanging and strip off a nibble.

Yes, you would have to grow up down on the New Meadows to enjoy this treat. I like to think it was a very good time.

★It came as a shock to me when a friend remarked, after reading every word in my first cookbook, "There isn't a thing about cooking smelts!" Probably the reason I decided to have the fun of writing a second cookbook was so I might talk about smelts.

It is hard to realize that a born and bred State-of-Mainer could forget such an important part of wintertime eating in our state. After all, you only need to take a ride on a winter's day and see the smelt shacks that dot the frozen rivers in many parts of Maine. If men, and women too, arrive at work on winter mornings looking a little bleary-eyed, it is almost certain they spent many hours in a smelt shack fishing for the next night's supper. If you catch your own, they are that much sweeter.

TO PREPARE AND COOK SMELTS

Place a piece of wax paper on a cutting board, place smelt on it, cut off head with a sharp knife. Cut along abdomen, using kitchen shears, remove entrails. Using your thumb, completely clean the smelt. Leave tail on, but use shears to cut off fins. Rinse fish thoroughly, wipe dry.

This is where Maine cooks differ in the way they cook smelts. You may fry them, broil them or bake them. You may roll them in a mixture of seasoned cornmeal. You may combine flour with cornmeal and season it. You may use a commercial preparation for dredging the fish. Or you may leave them plain.

You may fry them in salt pork fat, in melted margarine or butter or in oil. If you fry them, do it gently on one side until done, then turn and complete the other side. If you decide to bake them, use a shallow, buttered pan, in a hot oven of 450 degrees, 5 minutes on a side. If you prefer, you may broil them.

Isn't it nice to have a choice? No matter how you cook them, they are delicious and very much a part of the wintertime scene in Maine.

★Haddock Smother is not a chowder but I suggest you serve it in soup plates. It is as old-fashioned as any recipe in this cookbook. If haddock is not available, substitute cod or hake. You will not notice much difference, anyway. You will like this on a chilly summer's day as well as the coldest day in winter.

DOWN EAST
HADDOCK SMOTHER

Buy amount of fish necessary for your size family. Wipe with paper toweling and salt lightly. Cook in as little water as possible in a shallow, broad-bottomed saucepan. Use cold water, bring to a gentle boil and cook until just done. "Cook it short," as we say when cooking fish. Add enough milk to just cover fish; add salt and pepper.

Cover top of fish with crackers. Originally, we used Kennedy's Commons, no longer available. You may be able to find common crackers; if not, use whole unsalted crackers, thicker than saltines. These crackers should be soaked lightly in cold water before being placed on top of the cooked fish. Do not use milk for soaking the crackers. It would toughen them. Use a slotted spoon to lift them from the water and place them on the fish.

Push the crackers down into the milk. Dot tops with butter; allow to simmer a few minutes, using a low heat. Serve in soup plates, topped with a dash of paprika.

A tossed salad will be the right accompaniment for this.

★This recipe has deep meaning for men of the Woodfords Club in Portland. Russ Foster, the steward there, finds the popularity of this delicious fish very gratifying. After all, it is his own recipe. He shared it with us in my Cooking Down East column and now everyone in Maine can know about Famous Baked Haddock.

RUSS FOSTER'S
FAMOUS BAKED HADDOCK

You can adapt this recipe according to the number of people you will be serving. For four people, use a 7 x 11-

inch casserole. Rinse and wipe 1½ to 2 pounds fresh haddock fillets. Place a layer of haddock in bottom of buttered casserole. Add a second layer of fillets, making certain you place them on the bottom layer so a thick end comes on top of a thin end of the fillet beneath. You will serve the cooked fish in squares, so you see what you need to achieve. There should be an even thickness of fish all over the casserole. Squeeze fresh lemon juice all over the fish. Do this between each layer, too. Add salt and pepper. Cover top with buttered crumbs. Try using half cracker crumbs and half packaged seasoned crumbs. Bake at 350 degrees for ½ to three-quarters of an hour. Serve in squares.

For two people, use 1 pound fillets and a loaf pan for baking to get desired thickness. Three pounds of fillets will serve 8 people generously. This is good company fare. May be prepared ahead, then brought from refrigerator an hour ahead of baking time.

CRISP OVEN FRIED FISH

1½ pounds fish (cusk, hake or haddock)
3 cups cereal flakes
1 tablespoon salt

1 cup milk
2 tablespoons melted butter

Cut fish into serving pieces, allowing about ¼ pound fish per person. Roll cereal flakes into fine crumbs. Add salt to milk. Dip fish in milk, then in crumbs, arrange on well-buttered baking sheet. Dribble melted butter over top of fish. Bake at 500 degrees (this is correct) for 15 to 20 minutes.

BAKED FISH STICKS

2 pounds fish sticks
Salt and pepper
½ stick margarine, melted

6 tablespoons flour
Milk

Cut fish sticks into 6 servings. Salt and pepper each piece. Place in buttered shallow 7 x 11-inch pan. Mix flour with melted margarine so it is a paste. Add bit more flour if needed. Spread paste on top of each serving of fish. Pour milk in pan so it comes up around fish. Bake at 350 degrees about 45 to 50 minutes or until the fish flakes when tested with a fork.

★Corned hake is an old Maine dish. It is remembered by many and it is amazing how Maine families cling to serving this old-fashioned dinner. It is delicious and you will like serving it to your own family. Corned hake, boiled potatoes, butter gravy or, if you prefer, salt pork gravy is good any time of year. Use buttered beets for a vegetable. Just maybe you will want to chop some raw onions, place in a bowl, sprinkle a bit of sugar on top, pour vinegar over them, allow to set. Come dinnertime, pass the bowl, and sprinkle a few onions on top of the hake.

Always popular, hake is growing in popularity in Maine. It is a less expensive fish, delicious used in a chowder. In fact, you would use it as you do any fish. Try dipping hake fillets in beaten egg, then crumbs, as this holds the fish together for pan frying. You may buy fillets or round hake, meaning it is whole. Corned hake is usually available in your fish market, but you are going to feel very old-fashioned if you corn your own.

DIRECTIONS FOR CORNING HAKE

Two and one-half to three pounds of hake will serve four people amply and should leave enough fish to make hash or fishcakes. Buy either fillets or a piece of round hake. Wipe fish, place in dish, sprinkle with salt on both sides, cover, place in refrigerator eight hours or overnight. Before using, drain fish but do not wash.

CORNED HAKE AND BOILED POTATOES

Pare potatoes, place in large saucepan with small amount of water. Do not salt. Cover pan and boil potatoes until nearly done; place drained hake fillets on top of potatoes, add dash of pepper if you wish. Cover, bring back to steaming point; lower heat, allow to simmer 10 to 15 minutes longer. If it is chunk of corned hake, allow about 20 minutes, test for doneness, taking care to cook only until it "flakes."

Try out (fry) salt pork scraps if you like, using fat to make salt pork gravy. The crispy pork scraps can be sprinkled on top of fish when served. If you prefer a butter gravy, why not make it as our Gardiner neighbor used to do it. These directions came from her.

BUTTER GRAVY

Scald one pint of milk in top double boiler placed over boiling water. Add ½ teaspoon salt to milk. Mix 2 tablespoons flour with cold water so mixture is thin, add to scalded milk, stirring constantly until thickened. Add piece butter or margarine, pepper to taste, and one cut-up, hard-cooked egg. Many oldtime cooks used to simply beat up the raw egg in a cup, add it to the thickened gravy, stir until well blended. Then, tiny pieces of the cooked egg were all through the gravy. Leftover gravy may be added to fish hash or fish cakes.

★Rarely will you find a recipe for fish hash in any of today's cookbooks. Probably you do not need a recipe. Maybe you would rather make fish cakes. But if you happen to have leftover fish and potatoes, either boiled or mashed, why not get out your heavy frypan and make hash. My mother was a great hand to make fish hash, probably because we ate a lot of fish. I'm sure she did not have a recipe.

FISH HASH

1½ cups cooked fish
2 cups mashed or boiled
   potatoes

¼ teaspoon pepper
Salt to taste
1 egg, beaten
2 tablespoons margarine

Combine leftover fish and mashed potato, or if it's leftover boiled potato, then chop fine with fish. Add pepper and salt, mix with beaten egg. Add some dry mustard if you wish. Melt 2 tablespoons margarine in heavy frypan, add hash, cover pan. Use foil if your pan has no cover. Fry, using a medium heat until browned on the bottom. Fold over and serve very hot. Serves 4. Corn meal muffins, sliced carrots and a tossed salad are good with fish hash.

★In case you wondered where the name finnan haddie originated, it gets its title from the reputation of haddock cured around Findon, Scotland. For a long time I used to think of it as strictly a New England kind of fish. Today, it isn't even haddock that is used for smoked fillets — the high price makes this prohibitive. Usually cod or hake is used and it is called smoked fillets. Several processing plants along the Maine coast smoke fillets. They are delicious and naturally are used like finnan haddie. Occasionally you will find finnan haddie in our markets. Sometimes the fillets have not been smoked but have been dipped in a colored, smoky liquid to give the same flavor. These are lighter in color and the color will come off in milk or water.

SMOKED FILLET CASSEROLE

1 to 1½ pounds smoked fillets	½ cup diced green pepper
Water or skim milk to cover fish	1 small onion, diced
	4 tablespoons flour
2 tablespoons margarine or butter	¼ teaspoon salt
	2½ cups milk

Cut fish in three or four pieces, place in large saucepan, cover with water or skim milk. Place over a low heat, let stand until fish is ready to flake. Drain. This could have been leftover cooked fillets, in which case you would eliminate this part of directions. While fish cooks, melt margarine or butter in saucepan, add green pepper and onion and cook over low heat until soft. Add flour, stir until smooth. Add salt and the milk, using a low heat; stir constantly until thickened.

Place the flaked fish in a buttered 2-quart casserole. Make certain any bones are removed. Turn the thickened sauce over the fish. Top with buttered crumbs. Bake at 350 degrees for about 25 minutes. Serves 6.

BROILED FILLET OF SOLE

Wipe fillets. Lay fish flat on aluminum foil in a broiler pan or shallow baking pan. Dot lightly with butter, season with salt and pepper. Place under broiler. Leave oven door ajar and broil about 6 or 7 minutes. Sole is thin and usually does not need to be turned during the broiling. Serve hot with wedges of lemon. If you do not have a broiler, then follow same procedure and bake at 400 degrees for 20 minutes.

★It is a Maine tradition on the Fourth of July to serve fresh salmon, fresh green peas and new potatoes for your family dinner. The custom persists and I have questions like, "My mother cooked her piece of fresh salmon in cheesecloth and it was steamed. How do I do this, so I may carry on the tradition in my own family?" Of course you want to do this. Chances are there was a vegetable garden in your own back yard, where your father took great pride in raising "peas for the Fourth." Mine did. Green peas are still ready for the Fourth in Maine.

It means planting them by Patriot's Day — April 19th. It is a kind of silent contest in Maine among gardeners. Any man is happy to announce, "We're having peas from our garden for the Fourth!" They will not be new Maine potatoes at this time of year but you will probably serve boiled potatoes. They will be new and they will have come from out-of-state.

FRESH SALMON FOR THE FOURTH

THE AMOUNT TO BUY

When buying fresh salmon allow one-half to three-quarters of a pound per person. To refrigerate, remove the fish from the wrappings, place on a plate or platter with a piece of wax paper over it. This allows for circulation of air. If storing cooked fish in your refrigerator, it should be completely covered.

TO PREPARE FOR COOKING

As with all fish, fresh salmon neeeds little seasoning. The flavor of fish is so delicate that seasonings and sauces tend to take away from it.

Keep in mind that lemon juice and fish are old time partners. If no fresh lemon juice is available, then add vinegar to the water in which fish is cooked. This makes the salmon more firm and helps to preserve the color, too. Salt is the only other seasoning needed.

TO STEAM FRESH SALMON

In a covered pan, put enough hot water to come up fairly well around the fish. Add one-half teaspoon salt and one tablespoon fresh lemon juice (or vinegar) to each quart water used. Wrap salmon in cheesecloth and lower into the water. Cover pan, bring to steaming point. Reduce heat and allow to simmer 8 to 10 minutes per pound.

If fish is cooked too rapidly, it loses both flavor and food value. So remember to cook just under the boiling point. When tested with fork and salmon is flaky, drain, carefully remove the cheesecloth and arrange the salmon on a heated platter. Serve immediately with boiled new potatoes, fresh peas and a bowl of creamy egg gravy.

EGG GRAVY

4 tablespoons margarine	½ teaspoon salt
4 tablespoons flour	2 cups milk
½ teaspoon pepper	3 hard-cooked eggs

Melt margarine in saucepan using a low heat. Stir in flour, salt and pepper. Add milk gradually while continuing to stir; cook over a low heat until thickened and smooth. Add shelled hard-cooked eggs that have been cut up or chopped. The gravy may be further enhanced by adding a bit of minced fresh parsley and a bit of fresh lemon juice.

You may prefer fresh salmon baked in milk. Salt the fish, place in shallow pan, add about ½ inch milk. Bake at 375 degrees, allowing 12 minutes to the pound or until fish "flakes" when tested with a fork. Use uncovered pan for this.

★It might be a can of salmon kept in the refrigerator that will solve your summertime dinner problem. A one-pound can of salmon will serve 4. Salmon colored pink, medium-red or red all has the same food value but if you decide to do this with a can of salmon, then red has the greatest eye appeal. Turn contents of can into a bowl, remove skin and bones, separate the salmon into big chunks, arrange on lettuce on a platter with wedges of lemon and dollops of mayonnaise. No muss, no fuss. The chilled salmon served with potato salad and frozen peas cooked by the following method is a simple dinner to prepare.

TO COOK FROZEN PEAS

Use pan with tight fitting cover and only enough cold water to cover bottom of pan. Turn frozen peas into pan, add salt, cover pan. Bring to steaming point, making certain it is a forceful steam; lower heat and cook 10 minutes. Drain most of water from peas, draining it all, if you wish. Add piece of butter or margarine, salt and pepper to taste and a pinch of sugar. Reheat, serve very hot. This is not according to most package directions. Many cooks like to add cream to the peas after they have been seasoned.

★As soon as it was learned I had another cookbook under-way the questions started. The one asked most often was, "Will you have lots of casserole recipes?" Of that you may be certain. You will find them all through each of the next five chapters. There will be a kind of casserole recipe to satisfy just about everyone. Like this recipe using a can of salmon.

SALMON SURPRISE

1 tall can red salmon	measured in soup can
(A 1-pound can)	One 4-ounce package
1 can cream of	potato chips
mushroom soup	3 slices onion, minced fine
Same amount milk	½ cup sliced ripe olives

Prepare salmon by removing skin, bones and breaking into large pieces. Place half this salmon in buttered 7 x 11-inch casserole. Sprinkle a bit of onion over this, half of the ripe olives, half of the potato chips that have been crumbled. Mix soup and milk and turn half of this over potato chips. Repeat but save other half potato chips for topping of casserole. Bake at 350 degrees for 45 minutes. Serves 4.

FISH IN CHEESE SAUCE

3 tablespoons margarine	1½ cups milk
3 tablespoons flour	One 8-ounce package sharp
½ teaspoon salt	cheddar cheese
¼ teaspoon pepper	2 pounds haddock, cooked
½ teaspoon dry mustard	Buttered crumbs

Melt margarine in saucepan. Add flour, salt, pepper and dry mustard. Blend together, then add milk slowly. Cook over low heat, stirring constantly until thickened. Cut up cheese, add to sauce, stir until melted. Fold in cooked fish. Cook fish gently in salted water, using a low heat until it flakes. Separate into bite-size pieces before adding to sauce.

Turn into 2-quart casserole, top with buttered crumbs. Bake at 325 degrees about 25 minutes. If you prefer, this may be cooked in top of double boiler, kept hot over simmering water, served in toast cups. Serves 6.

TO MAKE TOAST CUPS

Use fresh bread. Cut off crusts. Use muffin tins. Press each slice into tins so that 4 points stand up. No need to brush with butter. Bake at 400 degrees for 15 minutes or until brown. If you need several, allow to cool in pan, remove to cookie sheet. Continue to do this until you have number needed. The toast cups will hold their shape. Slide cookie sheet into oven for reheating.

★Scalloped oysters are always a treat. This recipe from our Winthrop friend whose cooking is well known in this part of Maine says the recipe was given to her by an elderly friend, a long time ago. Like everyone else, you are sure to agree this is a very special recipe.

SCALLOPED OYSTERS

1 pint oysters, drained, save 2 tablespoons liquor	Salt and pepper
½ cup dried bread crumbs	1 tablespoon sherry
1 cup rolled cracker crumbs	1 tablespoon cream
¼ cup melted butter	Buttered crumbs for top

Mix crumbs with butter, using a fork. Butter an 11 x 7-inch casserole. Place thin layer crumbs in bottom, then a layer of oysters. Add salt and pepper, more crumbs, oysters, then top with crumbs. In case you do not have enough crumbs for top, then do a few more.

Using a knife, make holes down through layers, taking care not to mix layers. Mix oyster liquor, naturally you will use all of it; just make certain you have 2 tablespoons. Using an egg beater (yes even for this small amount) beat liquor, sherry and cream. Pour mixture into holes. Bake at 400 degrees for 20 minutes. Serves 4.

★This has to be one of my favorite ways of cooking fish— fillet of sole with oysters. It is expensive and takes a while to prepare but if you are looking for exactly the right recipe for guests, this has to be it. The Maine cook who gave it to me was chairman of the Maine Women's Golf Association that year. She liked it, for it could be prepared ahead. We all like this, especially when guests are invited.

FILLET OF SOLE WITH OYSTERS

2 pounds fillet of sole	1 quart fresh mushrooms, sliced
1 cup chicken broth	
3 tablespoons butter	2 dozen oysters, plus liquor, or use Maine shrimp
2 tablespoons lemon juice	

Heat broth, butter and lemon juice, using a large skillet. When butter is melted add fillet of sole. Lay sole in broth, simmer just until tender, about 3 minutes. If pan does not hold all of sole, do separately, so you do not crowd it. Butter a 13 x 11-inch pan. Lay cooked fish in pan. Add sliced fresh mushrooms to broth, cover, cook about 5 minutes; remember mushrooms take very little cooking. Use canned, sliced mushrooms if fresh are not available.

Drain mushrooms, save broth. Arrange mushrooms on top of fish. Add 2 dozen oysters and liquor to broth and simmer long enough for edges of oysters to curl. If you use Maine shrimp, then simmer only until shrimp curl. Remove from broth, arrange on top of mushrooms. Measure broth. You should have 1 and ¾ cups; if not, reduce amount by simmering. You will make a sauce with this broth.

TO MAKE SAUCE

5 tablespoons butter
½ cup flour
1 and ¾ cups fish broth
1 cup light cream or
    evaporated milk
Salt and pepper to taste

6 tablespoons grated
    parmesan cheese
3 tablespoons minced
    parsley
1 tablespoon grated onion
1 cup buttered soft
    bread crumbs

Melt butter, add flour, blend together; add fish broth and light cream slowly, stirring constantly. Cook over low heat until thickened. Add cheese, parsley, onion, salt and pepper to taste. Pour over contents in casserole. Top with buttered soft bread crumbs. Bake at 350 degrees for 30 minutes or until bubbly. Serves 8.

CRAB SOUFFLE

1 can or ½ pound fresh
    crabmeat
4 slices bread, diced
½ cup finely diced celery
½ small onion, minced
1 tablespoon diced
    pimiento

¼ cup mayonnaise
1½ cups milk
2 eggs, beaten
½ cup cream of mush-
    room soup
Freshly grated cheese

Dice bread, place half in buttered 1½ quart casserole. Spread crabmeat over this. Mix mayonnaise, celery, onion and pimiento; turn over crabmeat. Mix milk, beaten eggs with soup, turn over all. Bake at 325 degrees for 15 minutes. Sprinkle top with grated cheese, add paprika. Continue baking 1 hour longer. Serves 4 generously.

SEAFOOD NEWBURG

½ pound scallops
1 pound frozen Maine
  shrimp
¾ pound haddock
½ cup butter
4 tablespoons flour

2 cups milk
3 egg yolks
1 teaspoon salt
A shake or two of paprika
1 tablespoon lemon juice
6 tablespoons sherry

Cook the scallops, frozen Maine shrimp and haddock, taking care not to overcook. Drain. Prepare sauce as follows: melt butter in saucepan, add flour, mix well; add milk slowly, continuing to stir and cook over low heat until sauce thickens. This will take about 5 minutes.

Beat egg yolks. Add small amount thickened sauce to egg yolks. Blend, then slowly add egg yolk mixture to remaining sauce. Still using low heat, cook until sauce thickens. Add seasonings, add lemon juice and wine. Carefully fold in cooked fish. Turn mixture into a buttered 2-quart casserole. Top with buttered crumbs. Bake at 350 degreees about 20 minutes or until bubbly. Serves 6.

CANNED SEAFOOD CASSEROLE

One 6½ ounce can
  crabmeat
One 6½ ounce can lobster
One 5 ounce can medium
  shrimp
3 cups cooked rice
½ teaspoon pepper

1 can cream of celery soup
1 cup milk
2 tablespoons minced
  parsley
½ cup shredded
  cheddar cheese
½ cup buttered crumbs

Pick over crabmeat and lobster meat, if you can find the canned lobster meat. It is still being canned in Maine but is hard to find. You may just substitute another can of shrimp. Leave shrimp whole, devein if necessary. Mix cooked rice, soup mixed with milk, parsley and pepper, then combine gently with the fish. Turn into 2-quart casserole. Top with shredded cheese mixed with buttered crumbs. Bake at 350 degrees for 30 minutes or until bubbly hot. Serves 6.

★The Maine cook who gave me this recipe operated a restaurant in Gardiner. The good food served by this cook and her husband will long be remembered. Another of her recipes appears in my first cookbook. It wouldn't seem right not to share her Seafood Rarebit with you in this book. At the time she gave me this recipe, she said, "I have used this recipe for years. It is especially good to make ahead for a late supper. It is good warmed up."

SEAFOOD RAREBIT

In top of double boiler:
Melt 2 tablespoons butter
   or margarine
Add 2 tablespoons flour
½ teaspoon dry mustard
Salt and pepper to taste

Stir in:
1 cup finely cut
   sharp cheese
½ cup finely chopped
   green pepper
1 egg, beaten
¾ cup light cream or milk

Stir and cook until smooth and thick, over boiling water.

In a separate saucepan heat 1 can undiluted tomato soup with a pinch of soda until soup gets bubbly. Add to mixture in top of double boiler, continuing to stir. Then add:

1 can shrimp or 1 cup
   fresh shrimp
Or, 1 can crabmeat or
   1 cup fresh crabmeat

Or 1 can lobster meat or
1 cup fresh lobster
Or one 8-ounce can tuna
Or 1 cup any cooked fish

Isn't this an easy recipe to concoct? So many choices, too. You may serve this rarebit on crackers, rusk, toast points, rice, or in your favorite manner.

This is spelled rarebit, not to be confused with a Welsh Rabbit, which of course is something else.

★Old-fashioned Clam Pie is sometimes made with pota-toes, but most Maine cooks favor a clam pie that has nothing that takes away from the delicate clam flavor. Preferably, you will use fresh clams in making this delicious old Maine recipe.

OLD-FASHIONED CLAM PIE

Pastry for a 2-crust pie   Salt and pepper
1 pint fresh clams   1 tablespoon flour or
2 slices salt pork   enough to thicken
1 slice onion, minced   clam mixture

Use a spider and try out the salt pork, remove pork scraps. Add small amount of onion, cook until soft. Chop clams, not too fine. Add to fat and onion, cook gently about 5 minutes. Add flour to thicken; make certain mixture is hot. Add salt and pepper to taste.

Using 9-inch pie plate, line with pastry. When I turn a hot filling into a lower pastry, I like to have the top all rolled, ready to place over filling. Turn filling into pastry. Cut 3 slits in top pastry, place on pie. Flute edges. Bake at 400 degrees 15 minutes; lower to 325 degrees, continue baking about 25 minutes longer. Serve very hot. Serves 4.

★Having canned minced clams in your cupboard means you can do interesting things like stuffed clams. Or you could make a clam whiffle. You will find it good insurance against any kind of weather to have them on hand.

STUFFED CLAMS

Serves 2

One 7-ounce can minced   2/3 stick margarine
  clams   1 teaspoon Worcestershire
Same amount freshly rolled   sauce
  cracker crumbs,   Pepper
  measured in can

Melt margarine, add to crumbs. Drain clams and mix with buttered crumbs. Add Worcestershire sauce and pepper, taste for seasoning, add salt if you wish. Spoon into shells or small shallow casseroles. This will make a supper dish for 2. If served for a first course, use smaller shells and this amount will serve 4. Bake at 350 degrees for 20 minutes.

CLAM WHIFFLE

12 single saltine crackers
1 cup milk
2 eggs, beaten
¼ cup butter or margarine, melted
One 7-ounce can minced clams
¼ teaspoon Worcestershire sauce
1 teaspoon chopped green pepper
2 teaspoons chopped onion
Dash of salt and pepper

Crumble crackers and soak in milk for a few minutes, combine with other ingredients, adding beaten eggs last. Pour into greased 1½ quart casserole, place in shallow pan of hot water. Bake at 350 degrees, uncovered, for 40 minutes. Serves 4.

AN AMAZING LOBSTER NEWBURG

¾ pound lobster meat
½ cup sherry
2 tablespoons butter
2 tablespoons flour
2 hard-cooked egg yolks
1½ cups cream, plus
¼ cup milk
Pinch of nutmeg
Pinch of cayenne pepper
Salt to taste

Soak cooked lobster meat cut in bite-size pieces in sherry for 2 to 3 hours in refrigerator. Make a paste of softened butter, flour and the hard-cooked egg yolks that have been rubbed through a sieve. Use a heavy iron skillet, combine this paste with cream, milk, nutmeg and cayenne pepper. Add salt later.

Use a low heat, stir sauce until quite thick. Drain sherry from lobster meat, add to sauce, continue stirring and cooking until it is thick. Add lobster meat. Stir until hot.

Amazingly, this is better made the day before serving and stored in the refrigerator. Heat and serve on toast points.

BAKED SCALLOPS

1 pint scallops. If large, cut in halves or quarters. Dip each in flour, seasoned with salt and pepper. Let set a few minutes. Then dip each in beaten egg to which 1 tablespoon cold water has been added. Let set a few minutes.

Dip or roll each thus treated scallop in finely pulverized corn flakes. Arrange in large baking dish or on a cookie sheet that has been lightly buttered.

Bake 30 minutes at 350 degrees. Serves 4.

The dipping in flour and the "letting set" helps the crumbs adhere to the scallops, thus giving the appearance of nicely fried scallops—without the fat.

This tartar sauce is good to serve with the baked scallops or any fish where it is needed.

TARTAR SAUCE

1 cup mayonnaise	2 tablespoons chopped
½ teaspoon minced onion	stuffed olives
½ teaspoon minced parsley	1 teaspoon vinegar
¼ cup finely chopped dill	Dash of black pepper
pickles	

Combine, refrigerate in covered jar. Serve on piece of lettuce leaf.

SAVORY SCALLOPS
SERVED ON TOAST

1¼ pounds scallops	1/3 cup mayonnaise
1 teaspoon vinegar	½ teaspoon thyme
2 tablespoons butter	Salt to taste
2 tablespoons flour	Buttered toast

Parboil scallops in water that does not come quite up over them. Add vinegar. Keep water just under boiling, cook scallops just until they turn white. They cook quickly and overcooking toughens them. Drain and reserve the liquor.

Cut scallops into quarters. To scallop liquor add enough water to make 1 and 1/3 cups liquid in all.

Melt butter in separate saucepan, add flour, stir and blend. Add scallop liquor gradually, continuing to stir and cook over low heat. Add mayonnaise slowly, as soon as sauce thickness. Add cut-up scallops, thyme and salt. Heat through but do not boil. After combining all ingredients it will be best to keep this in top of double boiler over water kept just under boiling point. Serve on toast or in toast cups. This recipe serves 4 or 5. You might increase the amount of liquid to 2 cups, increase flour and butter to 4 tablespoons, use ½ cup mayonnaise, use same amount of scallops, and serve 6.

★This casserole recipe includes scallops as well as fish, also frozen cream of shrimp soup. This is another do ahead recipe which is well liked by all cooks.

LUNCHEON SEAFOOD CASSEROLE

1 stick margarine, melted
1 cup cracker crumbs
1 cup scallops, cut small
and parboiled 5 minutes
1 pound haddock or other
fish, cooked gently and
flaked. Save 2/3 cup of
the liquor from haddock

1 can undrained minced
clams
1 can frozen shrimp soup,
thawed
Small onion, finely minced
Salt and pepper

Mix margarine and crumbs. Set aside. Combine cooked scallops, haddock, clams and onion. Using one-half of the crumb mixture, combine with fish. Season lightly.

Combine thawed soup and haddock juice, mix with fish, taste again for seasoning. Turn into 2-quart casserole. Refrigerate if you wish. Before baking, cover top with remaining buttered crumbs. Bake at 350 degrees for 40 minutes. Serves 8.

★It was the longest time ago that I used this excellent method for cooking halibut in my column, "Cooking Down East." The recipe came from the Maine Department of Sea and Shore Fisheries.

HALIBUT BAKED
IN A COVERED DISH

2 pounds halibut, prefer- ably in one chunky piece 2 tablespoons soft butter or margarine	¼ teaspoon pepper ¼ teaspoon paprika Dash of salt Fresh grating of nutmeg

Have fish at room temperature. Combine butter, pepper, salt, paprika and nutmeg. Rub both sides of fish with it. Place fish in an ovenproof dish, cover with foil. Bake at 325 degrees until fish flakes; time depends upon shape. The general rule is 20 minutes for 1-inch thick fish, 30 minutes for 2-inch thick and 35 minutes for 3-inch thickness. 2 tablespoons water may be added while cooking. Place fish on a hot platter.

For a tasty sauce melt 3 tablespoons butter or margarine, add 2 tablespoons chopped pickles, 1 teaspoon chopped parsley, 1 teaspoon chopped chives and ½ teaspoon salt. Pour over fish. Makes 4 to 6 servings.

★The Bailey Island Tuna Tournament makes Maine tuna country. At Bailey Island during the summer months, it is not uncommon to have one or more tuna fish on the wharf daily being weighed and prepared for market. The appearance of fresh Maine tuna in our fish markets is a welcome sight. Usually low in price and considered a great treat, fresh tuna is served by Maine cooks as long as it is available.

TO COOK FRESH TUNA

Fresh tuna steaks are red and look exactly like beef steak. Again, "cooking it short" applies. Usually, Maine cooks fry fresh tuna or it is broiled. Remember, only until it changes color is enough. Because it is oily, many cooks parboil it first. You may prefer broiling it, under these circumstances, brushing it with melted butter or margarine and using fresh lemon juice for tartness and good flavor.

★Tuna is horse mackerel and this all leads up to one of Maine's most popular fish — mackerel. Best of all is tinker mackerel. If you have ever fished for mackerel, found your boat in a "school," only had to drop your line with a jig hook over the side of the boat, hauling them in so fast you stood ankle-deep because the half-barrel was overflowing, then the joy of sharing and eating them is very great.

You can buy them in your markets, from someone who might call at your door, or maybe the fishman still calls in your town. If a friend calls with an offer of mackerel he has caught, then be sure to accept them, for his joy is sharing them.

If you have never eaten tinker mackerel, I'm sorry. Tinkers are the babies, weighing not over a pound. There isn't another fish like it. They are simple to cook. Just allow enough per person.

TO COOK TINKER MACKEREL

They may be fried or broiled and they may be baked in milk the way people like to cook larger mackerel. Cook them as simply as possible. No sauce of any kind, for they are too delicious as they come out of the frypan or from the broiler.

Use salt pork fat or butter or margarine. Cook them just as they are or roll them in flour or a combination of flour and cornmeal. Cooks like the commercial preparations too, for dredging fish for frying. Season with salt and pepper.

Once the tinker mackerel have been cleaned, you may decide to cook them whole, because of their size. Yet, many people like to split them. No matter what you do, keep the cooking simple.

★Baking mackerel in milk is the Maine way of cooking this popular fish. Again, no other seasoning except salt and pepper and the moistness of milk; oh well, a few dots of butter.

MACKEREL BAKED IN MILK

Once the mackerel has been split and cleaned, arrange in a glass baking dish. Season with salt and pepper, dot with butter, pour milk in pan so it comes up to depth of fish but not over it. Bake at 350 degrees for 40 minutes.

★Do you ever watch the way canned tuna disappears from the grocer's shelves? It makes you aware that it is a necessary part of meal planning, both from the economy standpoint and from its many uses; all easy ones, too. Tuna Divan does not sound State-of-Maine-ish but we like everything about it.

TUNA DIVAN

One 10-ounce package
   frozen broccoli stalks,
   cooked and drained
Two 6½-ounce cans white
   meat tuna, water-packed,
   drained, separated into
   large chunks

Fresh lemon juice
1 can cheddar cheese soup
Buttered crumbs or
   buttered croutons

Use a buttered 7 x 11-inch casserole. Place drained, cooked broccoli stalks in casserole. In a separate bowl, mix drained tuna, about 1 tablespoon lemon juice and the soup. Spoon this mixture over the broccoli. Top with buttered crumbs or buttered croutons. Bake at 350 degrees about 25 minutes or until bubbly. Serves 6.

TUNA-NOODLE BAKE

One 8-ounce package wide
   noodles, cooked and
   drained
One 6½-ounce can tuna,
   of your choice, drained
¾ cup milk

1/3 cup pimientos, diced
1 can cream of mushroom
   soup
For topping:
Crumbled potato chips

Have you learned about cooking macaroni products the easy way? For this amount of noodles, boil 1 quart water in covered saucepan. Add salt. Add noodles, stirring constantly; bring to a boil, continue stirring for 2 minutes. Cover pan. Remove from heat. Let stand 10 minutes. Stir, then drain. Easy? Never boils over, either.

Combine cooked noodles, tuna that has been cut-up, milk and soup that have been mixed together, diced pimiento, and add some pepper if you wish. No salt needed. Turn into buttered 1½ quart casserole. Top with crumbled potato chips. Bake at 350 degrees about 35 minutes. Serves 4.

Do you have a problem keeping pimiento once it has been opened? Simply turn some vinegar on top of it in jar, cover, place in refrigerator. It keeps for weeks.

★Maine sardines — the little fish with the big flavor. Tins of sardine are what you take along on a trip — in your survival box. No family should ever go away from home for a few days and not include a small carton of foods for any emergency. Tins of Maine sardines take up so little room and they pack so much needed food value. Don't forget the box of salted crackers.

The many ways to use sardines are unlimited. They combine well with cheese, lemon juice, onions, tomatoes, bread, milk, potatoes. So there is no limit to what you may achieve if you have tins of Maine sardines stored in your cupboard.

DELUXE MAINE SARDINE SANDWICH

3 cans (4 oz.) Maine
  sardines
6 frankfurter rolls
Barbecue sauce or
  cocktail sauce

3 tablespoons butter or
  margarine
6 slices Swiss cheese
6 onion slices, if you
  wish

Cut rolls almost in half, lengthwise. Place opened rolls on a cookie sheet, spread with melted butter, place under broiler. Toast, spread other side with butter, toast, also.

Lay 3 sardines on each sandwich half, spoon barbecue sauce over sardines. Add onion slices if you wish, lay slice Swiss cheese on top. Place under broiler until cheese melts. Serves 6. These are served hot and you will find this one of the most delicious sandwiches you will ever eat. If you do not have a broiler, toast the rolls, assemble sandwich, then bake at 425 degrees for 12 to 15 minutes.

MAINE SARDINE DIP

One 4-ounce can Maine
   sardines
One 8-ounce package
   cream cheese
1 tablespoon milk
2 teaspoons grated onion
1 tablespoon Worcester-
   shire sauce

1 ½ tablespoons lemon
   juice
Salt and pepper to taste
2 tablespoons chopped
   parsley

Drain sardines, break into small pieces. Soften cream cheese, mix with milk. Combine all ingredients except parsley. Mix thoroughly. Chill. Sprinkle with parsley. Serve with chips, crackers or crispy raw vegetables.

★Maine shrimp — that delightful shellfish with its delicate flavor and texture — appeared in the icy waters of the Gulf of Maine to change and enhance the eating habits of many families. Not always this abundant, Maine shrimp brought a whole new seafood industry to our state.

The appearance of the pick-up trucks that dot our highways from early winter to the end of the shrimp season, selling Maine shrimp, are a welcome sight. Families buy them by the pound and by the bushel. They have them for supper and they freeze them. Come to think of it, there isn't any Maine shellfish that is easier to cook or to freeze. You may be as lazy as you wish about Maine shrimp, for you will find them in the frozen food section at your market, either frozen raw or frozen cooked. That is easiest of all, isn't it?

HOW MUCH MAINE SHRIMP
TO BUY

If you buy shrimp in the shell, you will get about half of what you start with. Two pounds of shrimp in the shell will give you one pound of the shrimp.

A one-pound package of frozen shrimp will yield 2 cups of shrimp, either fresh or frozen.

TO COOK MAINE SHRIMP
IN SHELL

Wash shrimp. Break off heads using your fingers. Use a covered kettle and about 1 inch boiling, salted water. Place shrimp in kettle. Cover, bring back to a boil. Cook not more than 2 minutes after boiling point is reached. Drain, cool, remove shrimp meat by peeling off shells.

TO COOK SHRIMP MEAT

Place shelled out shrimps in about ½ cup boiling water, to which has been added salt and a small amount of lemon juice or vinegar. Cover, bring back to steaming point. It takes not more than one minute of cooking for peeled, raw shrimp. If you would protect its delicate flavor, do not overcook.

FREEZING MAINE SHRIMP

The heads are snipped off, using your fingers. Wash shrimp in salted water, place shrimp in plastic container, cover tightly and into the freezer they go. That's it, nothing else. You freeze them in the shell, which acts as a protection and keeps them from drying out.

No brine, nothing else. A container of quart size will hold about 60 Maine shrimp. No need to thaw shrimp before cooking. Just drop the frozen shrimp into inch of boiling water, return to boil and cook three minutes.

Maine Chicken

*Strange to see how a good dinner and
feasting reconciles everybody*

CHAPTER THREE

Maine Chicken

Maine chicken provides many a showpiece dinner. This holds true whether you have your own family in mind or it is to be served to company.

This was the case even when you hark back to the days that chicken was a special treat reserved for Sunday dinner. But that was an entirely different kind of chicken. Most Maine farms kept a flock of laying hens. Unless you were so fortunate as to have a chicken that was just right for roasting, you were conjuring up ways of cooking fowl and roosters to make them more tender. We do not forget the miracle of the tenderness of those chicken pies or fricasseed chicken.

Today in our markets, Maine chicken is year-round. It is scientifically raised and the resulting tenderness of our chickens is well-known. It has been inspected for wholesomeness and graded for quality. You will find it one of the best buys at your market-place.

Today's cook is aware of the nutrition needs of her family. She knows chicken offers a generous amount of high-quality protein. It is low in calories, making it popular with all family members.

Regardless of how you choose to cook your bird, the results are sure to please. Maine chickens are plump, tender, meaty, delicately flavored birds that have been produced for your eating pleasure.

All this and we haven't even started to talk about cooking it to make it this showpiece we referred to. It could be the most formal of dinner parties you have in mind.

Or an informal buffet. You could tote it to a picnic or it could shine at a barbecue.

Regardless of how you choose to cook it, Maine chicken is certain to meet with a warm welcome from youngsters and grown-ups alike.

TO BUY CHICKEN

The bird you find in your market is ready to cook. This means the chicken has been cleaned inside and out. It is free of pin-feathers and is eviscerated — the head, feet and inedible organs have been removed before the bird was weighed for pricing. The giblets (liver, gizzard, heart) have been washed, trimmed and wrapped, and usually have been placed inside the body cavity. Chicken comes to you packed in many different ways; there is a pack for every cooking preference.

Cut-up chicken and chicken in parts offer maximum convenience for little more cost. A cut-up three pound chicken, for instance, may cost a little more than a three-pound whole bird, but very little in terms of the kitchen time you save.

Family preferences differ. If, for instance, your family prefers white meat, it may be more economical for you to buy chicken breasts. Although chicken parts cost a little more per pound, you save money with less waste.

You will need approximately ¾ pound of chicken per serving. A three-pound bird yields four servings; a two-pound bird yields two servings.

TO STORE CHICKEN

Chicken may be stored in a normally cold refrigerator for one to two days — no longer — before cooking. You will be wise to cut the tight wrap over the chicken in the supermarket tray, so air may get to the uncooked chicken for its short term of storage in the refrigerator. You may want to remove the uncooked chicken to a smaller platter or pie plate, covering it loosely with wax paper or plastic wrap for this short period of storage. Always make certain air is getting to uncooked chicken. If it is cooked chicken that is being stored, this needs to be completely wrapped.

TO FREEZE CHICKEN

Uncooked chicken may be frozen whole or in parts; cooked chicken also takes well to the freezer. Maximum storage time for chicken wrapped, frozen, and stored under the most favorable conditions is 12 months for uncooked chicken and six months for cooked chicken dishes, with the exception of fried chicken which keeps well for about four months.

Whether you use wraps or bags, make certain they are suitable for freezing food. Heavy-duty aluminum foil, cellophane-coated freezer paper, polyethylene freezer paper and plastic freezer bags are recommended. Whatever you use, make certain the air is pressed out of the package before sealing.

Cooked chicken with gravy or sauce should be packed in rigid containers with tightly-fitting lids.

Label your packages with date, kind of chicken or dish, weight and number of servings. It is a good idea to wrap together and freeze the number of parts you would normally be using.

Do not stuff whole chicken before freezing.

It is best to thaw the chicken in the refrigerator. To speed thawing, refrigerate on tray or plate. Whole frozen chickens under four pounds require 12 to 16 hours refrigerator time to thaw. To thaw chicken pieces, refrigerate for 4 to 9 hours.

★Chicken pie is very popular in Maine. This recipe that came from Searsport has a different kind of flavor. As you eat it, you will wonder why it is so good. it is such a simple recipe. You will probably decide as I did, that it has to be the crust. This same crust may be used for other hearty type pies.

SEARSPORT CHICKEN PIE

FILLING

3 cups cooked chicken, cut in large pieces

1 can cream of mushroom soup, undiluted

1 pimiento, diced fine

Mix all together and heat mixture. If pimiento is already diced in jar, use ¼ cup.

CRUST

2 cups sifted flour

1 teaspoon soda

2 teaspoons cream of tartar

½ teaspoon salt

½ cup vegetable shortening

1 egg

½ cup milk

Sift dry ingredients together, work in shortening using pastry blender. No blender? Then use 2 knives. Beat egg, combine with milk; add to dry mixture, using a fork for mixing. Divide mixture in half and roll out.

Have you tried 2 sheets of plastic wrap for rolling pastry? It works very well. Use damp cloth to wipe cooking counter, for this dampness keeps bottom plastic wrap in place on counter. Lay first sheet on counter. Lay pastry on it, then the top sheet of plastic wrap. Use rolling pin, roll to desired thickness. You may do the same thing with wax paper, or you will get out your bread board anyway.

Remove top sheet of wrap, turn pastry onto 10-inch pie plate. Roll out second pastry before filling lower crust with hot mixture. Fill bottom pastry with hot chicken filling. Cut 3 slits in top pastry, fit over hot filling, flute edges together. Bake at 400 degrees for 18 minutes. Cut into 6 pieces. Serve hot. It amazes me — this pie is always baked in the 18 minutes. Serve with mashed squash, cranberry sauce and celery.

TATER-DIPPED CHICKEN

One cut-up frying chicken
weighing 2 to 3 pounds
1 egg
2 tablespoons cold water

Seasoning of your choice
Dry potato flakes
½ stick margarine,
melted

Prepare cut-up chicken for cooking by washing and wiping dry. Melt margarine in shallow baking pan. Beat egg, add cold water. Dip chicken pieces in this. Season with salt, pepper and any other seasoning you like. Using packaged dry potato flakes, roll chicken in them so it is well covered. Lay prepared chicken in pan in melted margarine. Bake, uncovered, at 400 degrees for ½ hour; lower heat to 350 and bake about 45 minutes longer. Test for doneness. Serves 4.

CHICKEN-RICE CASSEROLE

2 cups coarsely cut-up
cooked chicken
2 cups cooked rice
1 small onion, chopped fine
4 hard-cooked eggs, sliced
½ cup slivered almonds

1 cup mayonnaise
2 cans cream of mushroom
soup, undiluted
2 tablespoons lemon juice
½ teaspoon salt
Buttered crumbs

Combine cooked chicken, cooked rice, onion, cooked egg slices and almonds. Mix mayonnaise, undiluted soup, lemon juice and salt. Combine two mixtures, turn into large buttered casserole. Cover. Place in refrigerator for 24 hours. Remove from refrigerator 1 hour before baking. Top with buttered crumbs. Bake, uncovered, at 350 degrees 45 to 60 minutes. Make certain it is all bubbly. Serves 8 to 10. Serve with raspberry gelatin salad for color, green beans, hot rolls. And for dessert, lemon meringue pie.

BAKED CHICKEN LEGS

6 chicken legs, disjointed
or cut so you have
12 pieces
Put flour, salt, pepper in
paper bag

3 eggs, beaten
About 20 saltine crackers,
rolled

Prepare 6 chicken legs by disjointing, so you have 6 legs and 6 thighs. Wash and wipe dry. Shake pieces of chicken in flour mixture.

Beat eggs, dip floured chicken pieces in it. Crush saltines, roll chicken in crumbs. Use large ungreased, shallow baking pan. Bake at 350 degrees for 1½ hours. After ½ hour of baking, baste occasionally with mixture of 1 stick margarine, melted and mixed with ½ cup water and juice of 1 lemon. This gives a delicious flavor to the baked chicken legs. Serves 6.

★A long time ago, I judged a chicken broiling contest under the Bowdoin Pines. Marketing specialists from the Maine Department of Agriculture were preparing the chicken barbecue. Hundreds wandered under the Pines or were eating the delicious chicken barbecue. It was for the benefit of a local hospital, so interest was high. It was made even more so because the contest was being staged by local doctors. Each had his own grill and each had his own favorite recipe for barbecuing chicken. Since I was the only judge, it was all up to me. The choice was not easy, yet One-Sauce, Two-Sauce I have always felt. was a delicious decision.

ONE-SAUCE, TWO-SAUCE
FOR
BARBECUED CHICKEN

Choose 2 to 3-pound broiler-fryer chickens, split for broiling. Prepare by washing and wiping dry. Brush with One-Sauce, place chickens on grill, skin side up. Turn every 10 minutes or so, brushing with sauce each time. After 45 minutes, Two-Sauce is brushed on and the broiling continued 15 minutes or so longer until chicken is very tender.

ONE-SAUCE

1 cup salad oil   ¼ cup lemon juice

TWO-SAUCE

1 clove garlic, finely minced	¼ teaspoon pepper
2 tablespoons brown sugar	1 cup pineapple juice
1 teaspoon salt	¼ cup salad oil
1 shake oregano	

★Sharing a recipe makes it very special and when you share your recipe you have kept for special occasions, then you give a little of yourself. Other people appreciate it so much. The wife of a Gardiner doctor felt that way about this chicken recipe.

MAINE CHICKEN SUPREME

6 large chicken breasts, left whole. Put these in a large kettle. Over them, pour

2 cans chicken broth	1 cup diced carrot
½ cup diced celery	1 small onion, diced

Cover kettle, bring to steaming point; lower heat, cook slowly about 1½ hours or until chicken is very tender. Remove chicken from kettle and cool until it may be handled. Remove meat from bones, keeping it in as large pieces as possible, tucking any pieces under, so you have 12 large servings. Arrange these in a large shallow casserole.

Meanwhile, cook down the broth left in kettle, leaving cover off and using medium heat. When about 1½ cups remain, put it through sieve. This is to be added to sauce that is poured over chicken.

Make a cream sauce:

3 tablespoons butter	2 cups light cream or
¼ cup diced green pepper	evaporated milk
3 tablespoons flour	2 tablespoons diced
½ teaspoon salt	pimiento
	1½ cups puree
	(from cooking chicken)

Melt butter, add green pepper. Cook until soft. Add flour and salt and stir until smooth. Add cream or, if you wish, evaporated milk; cook slowly, stirring constantly until thickened. Add puree, stir and cook about 5 minutes longer. Add diced pimiento. Cool. Pour sauce over chicken in casserole and refrigerate. When chilled, cover.

This is best when allowed to mellow for 24 hours before baking. Bring to room temperature, bake uncovered about ½ hour at 325 degrees or until bubbly. Serve with steamed rice. Serves 8 to 10 generously.

★Since we are constantly on the lookout for easy casserole recipes using left-over cooked chicken, it would be hard to find one you could enjoy more than the one that follows. Unless it is the one that follows that.

EASY CHICKEN CASSEROLE

6 slices fresh bread, buttered

1 small can mushrooms, undrained

1 cooked chicken breast

2 cans chicken noodle soup, undiluted

1 can cream of mushroom soup, undiluted

2 eggs

Butter slices of bread, cut into cubes. Not necessary to butter unless you wish. Place in buttered 2-quart casserole. Turn contents of can of mushrooms over bread cubes, Cut up cooked breast of chicken or equivalent into bite-size pieces, spread over mushrooms. Beat 2 eggs, combine with 3 cans soup, undiluted. Turn mixture over all. No seasoning in this recipe. Bake at 350 degreees for 50 minutes. Serves 6. You may prefer to set the casserole into a pan of hot water for baking. It will result in a smoother texture.

EASIEST CASSEROLE

2 cups left-over cooked chicken (or turkey)

1 can cream of mushroom soup

1 can Welsh Rarebit

One 10-ounce package frozen broccoli or asparagus

Buttered crumbs

Arrange layers of meat and thawed vegetable in buttered 7 x 11-inch casserole. Combine rarebit and soup, turn mixture all over top of meat and broccoli. Top sauce with buttered crumbs. Bake at 375 degrees for 30 minutes. Serves 4.

MOLDED CHICKEN LOAF

Two 6-ounce cans chicken or about 2 cups cut-up cooked chicken
½ cup celery, cut fine
1 can chicken with rice soup, undiluted

1½ tablespoons plain gelatin mixed in a little cold water, add enough boiling water to make 1 cup
3 tablespoons mayonnaise
Salt, pepper and paprika

Combine cut-up chicken with celery and undiluted chicken with rice soup, heated. Add gelatin mixture and mayonnaise, salt and pepper to taste, with a dash of paprika. Turn into small loaf pan that has been rinsed with cold water. Place in refrigerator overnight. Slice and serve. A wonderful warm weather dish.

★Toasted chicken salad rolls are a great favorite. This recipe may be used for filling in toasted hot dog rolls, or use it for party sandwiches between thin slices of white bread, the crusts trimmed off and saved for a bread pudding. If it is a party you have in mind, toast some pecans in melted margarine in a small frypan, cool slightly, chop fine and add. Not too many now, but oh, what flavor.

CHICKEN SALAD SANDWICH FILLING

When a recipe of this sort calls for cooked chicken meat, try to find a Bro-Hen, which is a plump, meaty laying hen, weighing from 4½ to 6 pounds. This will be cooked leisurely to provide tender meat which is exactly right for making sandwich filling.

Prepare for cooking. If you bought it whole, leave it that way. Place chicken or pieces in large kettle. Add 1 quart cold water, salt, pepper, a small onion, a stalk or two of celery and maybe half a carrot. Cover, bring to steaming point; lower heat, cook until very tender. This could take 2 to 3 hours; just make certain it is tender. Remove from kettle and cool to lukewarm. You may want to save the liquor and the chicken bones to make a soup.

If you remove chicken meat from the bones while it is still warm, you find it easier to do. But you will find the chicken meat easier to cut if it is cold, so place in refrigerator until cool. If using for party sandwiches, cut in smaller pieces than if it is to be used as a filling for salad rolls.

Cut up chicken, add a little salt, pepper, at least the juice of 1 lemon for this amount of chicken, a bit of Accent if you wish. Cover, place in refrigerator for overnight. The next day, mix with mayonnaise or salad dressing.

This amount of chicken will make filling for about 72 party-size sandwiches. Possibly you are making this to use in hamburg-type buns, untoasted. However, you will find the chicken salad rolls are far tastier if you spread with soft margarine, place on cookie sheet under broiler until toasted. Turn, spread other side and place under the broiler. Then fill with the chicken salad filling. Especially if you use bits of lettuce in the roll, it is nicer to do the toasting first.

★Nothing can be more of a showpiece for chicken than a large platter heaped high with this delicious way of preparing chicken salad. This is not a Maine recipe at all. A lot of people have retired in Maine from out-of-state; this is how the recipe came to us. It is sure to be one of your favorite ways of serving Maine chicken.

CHICKEN SALAD

3 cups cooked chicken cut in large chunks	1 cup mayonnaise—if you prefer, Miracle Whip
3 tablespoons lemon juice	¼ cup light cream or dairy sour cream
1 cup halved seedless green grapes	1 teaspoon dry mustard
1½ cups very thinly slivered celery	Dash of black pepper
1 cup slivered toasted almonds	½ teaspoon salt
	Dash of soy sauce
	½ teaspoon curry powder

Prepare cooked chicken, marinate with fresh lemon juice. Place bowl in refrigerator while preparing dressing.

Mix mayonnaise, cream, mustard, pepper, salt, as many dashes of soy sauce as you like, and the curry powder. Taste for seasoning. Mix with the marinated chicken, add halved green grapes, slivered celery and slivered almonds. Taste again for seasoning. Chill. Turn onto large platter on bed of lettuce, garnish with drained pineapple chunks, ripe olives and paprika. Serves 10.

CHICKEN A LA KING

4 tablespoons butter or
   margarine
1 cup sliced mushrooms
4 tablespoons flour
2 cups milk or chicken
   stock
½ teaspoon salt

¼ teaspoon pepper
2½ cups diced cooked
   chicken
1 cup frozen or canned
   peas
3 tablespoons diced
   pimiento

Lightly brown mushrooms in butter or margarine. Blend in the flour. Gradually stir in the milk or chicken stock. Cook in top of double boiler, stirring until thickened. Add chicken, cooked peas and pimiento. Season to taste and cook 10 minutes more. Serves 8. Serve in patty shells, toast cups or on toast points.

★This next chicken recipe is rightly named. It is a perfect recipe to prepare for guests. It is put together, covered, placed in the refrigerator for 24 hours, then baked. Could anything be easier? There is hardly any work to preparing it, either.

MAINE PARTY CHICKEN

4 good sized whole, boned
   chicken breasts
8 slices bacon
1 package dried beef or
   1 small jar

1 can cream of mushroom
   soup, undiluted
½ pint commercial sour
   cream

Divide each chicken breast in half, giving you 8 servings. Wrap each half with a piece of bacon. Using a buttered shallow 9 x 13-inch baking pan, cover bottom with thin slices dried beef. Arrange chicken breasts on dried beef. Mix soup and sour cream. Spoon over all. Cover pan, refrigerate 24 hours. Bring to room temperature before placing in oven. Bake uncovered at 275 degrees for 3 hours. This long, slow cooking is fine when guests are expected. If you are serving men, they are sure to be back for seconds. Better make that 12 half chicken breasts.

★If you long for the old-time flavor of chicken, the recipe that combines easy cut-up chicken with undiluted cream of chicken soup gives an amazingly good substitute. It could be an answer to your wish. If you combine two kinds of chicken, then you get the following title.

CHICKEN-CHICKEN

3-pound chicken, cut up
1 can cream of chicken
  soup, undiluted
½ cup cold water
1 teaspoon prepared
  mustard, Dijon type
Black pepper

Wash pieces of chicken, remove any extra pieces of skin, fat, the wing tips; wipe dry and place in a casserole. Mix soup, water and mustard (Dijon is a French, light brown colored mustard but do not buy a new jar to get this kind — use what you have). Turn this all over pieces of chicken. Grate fresh pepper or shake pepper over sauce. Cover casserole tightly, use foil if casserole does not have cover. Bake at 275 degrees for 3 hours or you could use 250 degrees for as long as 4 hours.

BAKED CHICKEN
FRENCH STYLE

One 3-pound chicken,
  left whole
Wash, prepare for baking,
  wipe. Rub inside with
  following mixture:
1 teaspoon salt
1 teaspoon Accent
½ teaspoon thyme
2 teaspoons dried parsley

After seasoning, stuff bird
  with celery tops and place
  one whole peeled onion in
  cavity
Rub with margarine. Push
  legs down, tie together,
  then to tail
Place chicken in casserole
  or small roaster, cover

Bake at 375 degrees for 30 minutes, add
Small white or regular onions, peeled
¼ cup dry sherry
1 teaspoon salt

Cover, bake 30 minutes longer. Remove cover, bake until chicken is tender. Baste often with juices. Total baking time, about 2½ hours. Serves 4.

★Men are part of the picture in the recipes that are in this cookbook. Red's Chicken is one of the easily concocted ways that appeal to men. It is easy to prepare, simmers slowly in electric frypan or covered skillet on the stove, and is delicious. Besides, the recipe is Red's specialty.

RED'S CHICKEN

Boned chicken breasts
from 2 fryers
Seasoned coating mix
for browning chicken
Oil for browning
1 cup white wine

1 cup chicken broth,
prepared by using 3
chicken bouillon cubes in
1 cup boiling water
1 small can mushrooms,
undrained
1 can small white onions,
drained

Use electric frypan or covered, large frypan on stove. Roll boned chicken breasts in seasoned coating mix and fry in about 4 tablespoons oil. Turn wine and chicken bouillon over chicken. Add canned mushrooms and liquid. Add drained small, white onions. Cover, simmer very slowly until chicken is tender. Actually this does not take very long but that long, slow, simmering is what blends all these delicious flavors. Even for as long as 2 hours.

His wife suggests lemon rice to accompany this chicken. Just substitute 2 or 3 tablespoons lemon juice in place of some of the water in cooking rice.

TO COOK RICE. Use twice as much cold water as rice. Add salt. Cover pan. Place over low heat, right from the beginning. Allow to cook 50 to 60 minutes. It never boils over. Nor does it need to be rinsed. Try this same proportion, using a covered casserole if your oven is in use. At 350 degrees, the rice will be cooked in slightly under an hour's time, ready to be brought to the table. 1 cup dry rice and 2 cups water will serve 4 to 6 people.

★You thought that was a big motel in the distance, the first time you traveled along one of Maine's highways and saw the blazing lights of a broiler house over on a hillside, didn't you? People have, you know. Just Maine chicken growing, that's all.

Meats

God sends meat, and the Devil sends cooks

CHAPTER FOUR

Meats

It is good to know that throughout Maine there is a trend toward the preservation of old country stores. We like to think young people will know the enchantment of visiting such a store. Some of these old stores have been modernized in part, keeping a section that is the country store of long ago. Others are of the museum type.

The State Museum in Augusta has such a store. It is named Brown's General Store. Besides being of the museum variety, it sells items like old-fashioned crackers, pickles, cheese and the penny candies we like to remember. You will find this so in other country stores you chance to visit in Maine. Dry beans are one of the popular items for sale. The mere mention of an old country store and people are off to visit it.

Walking into Brown's General Store the first time, I could not help but remember A. I. Snow's Store in Brunswick. I remember it well, for when I was in the 5th grade, we moved from the farm to town and lived right next door to "A. I's," on the second floor of the lovely old General Chamberlain house.

It was easy to drop into "A. I.'s." That was what everyone called him. His store was in a fine location — not only was it easily accessible to townspeople but to folks from out in the country. There were hitching posts where farmers could hitch their horses and teams. Of course, they made deliveries all over town in those days. You called your order into the store and our oldtime store keepers knew exactly what each family liked and usually delivered at about the same time each day.

To step inside "A. I's" and take a look 'way back was to get a view of stores no longer in existence. Oldtime grocery stores were wonderful to behold with their bins filled to overflowing, and with the pickle barrel, big rounds of cheese, tub butter, smoked herring hanging from sticks, the hogshead of molasses, and the hand-operated coffee mill that gave off its delightful aroma.

There was the less interesting but familiar smell of kerosene, cracked corn and yellow soap. They were all a part of a life now gone.

The candy counter was popular — made even more so by a very understanding young woman who patiently counted out 5 for a penny, 10 for a penny.

"A. I." had several clerks; he needed them for he was a checker player. If you dropped in and the clerks were all busy and "A. I." was deep in a checker game, you waited until the game was finished, if you wanted to see him. This never made any difference to any one as "A. I." was too deeply loved and respected. Especially by children.

To remember those days is to recall that important part of any old store — the meat block. They were very worn from so much usage. You can picture them, all scrubbed, ready for the next cutting of meat. The meat saw usually hung above, and attached alongside the old meat block a wooden rack held the meat cleaver, boning knives and butcher knives. Of course it held a steel for sharpening knives. A wooden box beneath held the waste bones. Always, there was sawdust on the floor.

One meat man I knew hummed a little tune as he poured a tiny amount of denatured alcohol on the meat block, struck a match to it and used the tiny flame for singeing chickens. When the task was completed, he threw a towel onto the flame to put it out.

Whether your choice of meat is one of the finer cuts or of the more humble variety, learn to respect the advice of your meat man. He is the one who knows and he will like to advise you. After that, it will be up to you to cook it properly so its goodness will be maintained, for it is the backbone of your meal.

★Fresh pork smother — a country dish. Doesn't that sound good? That is exactly the way my older friend described it when she sent the recipe. Smothers have long made the local scene in Maine. They are not confined to just fish and clams. If you wanted to, you could make a beef or a chicken smother. Pork smother is certain to become a family favorite. Our friend from Warren tells us it was used over the years by her grandmother, then her mother. All these years she has made pork smother, too. In Maine, we call this a heritage recipe.

FRESH PORK SMOTHER

Select the number of fresh pork spareribs you need for your family. You will find two kinds available in the markets; regular fresh spareribs or cut country style, which will have more meat on them.

This is a meal to be cooked on top of the stove in a heavy, covered pan. If you have an electric frypan, then that is exactly what you will use.

Wipe spareribs and place in bottom of heavy, covered dish on surface of your range or use electric frypan. Slice one onion over pork, turn about 1½ inches water into pan, add salt and pepper. Cover pan, bring to steaming point lower heat and simmer about 2 hours.

Add pared potatoes and a few slices of turnip. "For a bit of color and to add pepperiness," our friend tells us. Make certain you have at least an inch of water in pan when you add the vegetables. Add salt and pepper. Return the cover, bring back to steaming point, cook about 1 hour longer. About 15 minutes before serving comes the fun part. You are going to add dumplings.

DUMPLINGS

2 eggs, beaten	2 teaspoons baking
2/3 cup milk	powder
2 cups sifted flour	½ teaspoon salt

If your family is small, then halve this recipe. Sift dry ingredients together. Combine beaten eggs and milk. Add to dry ingredients. No fat in recipe. Drop by spoonfuls onto potato and spareribs. Cover pan, leave heat as it is, cook 15 minutes, WITHOUT PEEKING. Do not be concerned if there is not much liquid in pan when you add the dumplings; merely drop them on the potatoes and meat. At the end of 15 minutes they will look like puffy white mushrooms. Arrange this delicious dinner on a platter, with a dash of paprika added for color.

PORK CHOPS IN A LOAF

To prepare pork chops in this way, use a 9 x 5 x 3-inch loaf pan. The idea is to place a chop, standing, in one end, then dressing, and so on. Turned onto a platter after baking; served with sauerkraut it is a meal to remember. If, instead, you served Maine applesauce, that would also be a remembered dinner.

To serve 6 people, prepare the following amount of dressing.

2 slices onion, diced	½ teaspoon sage
¼ cup diced celery	1 teaspoon salt
2 tablespoons margarine	½ teaspoon pepper
2 cups fresh bread crumbs	2 tablespoons chopped parsley

Cook onion and celery in margarine that has been melted in frypan. Do not brown them. Add crumbs and seasonings. Toss lightly. You may need just the smallest amount of water to make this cling together. You may decide to use packaged stuffing anyway, which is delicious.

Use a loaf pan, place a pork chop in one end of pan. Place some dressing between that chop and the next one. Keep adding chops and dressing until the pan is full. End with a chop. Bake at 325 degrees for 1½ hours. Turn from pan onto platter for serving.

If you want to bake potatoes at this same temperature and time, prick potatoes with a long-tine fork. When baking potatoes at this low a temperature, it is best to place them on a piece of foil on the oven rack. The lower temperature sometimes makes the potatoes sizzle out the holes into the oven.

★Fresh sauerkraut from Waldoboro is famous in our state. You will find it in our markets from fall through the winter months. Sauerkraut has healthful qualities and these were recognized as far back as 200 B. C. when, history records, it was served to the laborers working on the Great Wall in China. To retain its full flavor, serve it raw or barely heated through. Cooking makes sauerkraut milder. If fresh sauerkraut is not available in your market, then canned is delicious.

TO COOK SAUERKRAUT

2 tablespoons butter or bacon drippings	1 quart fresh sauerkraut or
½ cup minced onion	Large can sauerkraut

This is in case you want to season the sauerkraut. It happens we like ours plain. Cook minced onion in butter or bacon fat just until it is soft, add sauerkraut, 1 or 2 tablespoons brown sugar and 1 teaspoon celery seed. Mix together, turn into covered casserole, place in oven the last 45 minutes the pork chop loaf is baking at 325 degrees.

If oven is not in use, cook sauerkraut on top of range, adding about 1 cup water. Cover pan and simmer on a low heat for 45 minutes. Maybe you will like just black pepper freshly grated over the top of the cooked sauerkraut, too.

★Every so often a cooking method comes along that erases any doubts in people's minds about the result they want. If it is a rib roast of beef that is to be cooked, then it is imperative that we have good results. From the economy angle as well as the pride of having guests say, "You never ate any thing like her roast beef." When our close friend, Kay, shared her method for roasting a rib roast of beef, she changed the entire picture in Maine. So now we follow her directions to the letter. And not only do we expect perfect results every time, we get them.

FOOLPROOF RIB ROAST OF BEEF

One standing rib roast of beef, any number of pounds
Salt and pepper

Plan your day so you will not need your oven for anything else. You are going to roast the beef in the morning for one hour. You must leave it in the oven all day and the oven door must not be opened. There are TWO STEPS to be followed in preparation.

STEP I

IMPORTANT: Let the roast stand at room temperature for one hour before placing in oven.

Preheat oven to 375 degrees. Rub roast with salt and pepper, place on rack in shallow pan, RIB SIDE DOWN. Roast for one hour at 375 degrees. After the hour, turn the oven switch OFF. DO NOT OPEN THE OVEN DOOR. The larger the roast, the longer time it continues to cook after the oven is turned off.

STEP II

About 30 to 40 minutes before serving time, again turn oven to 375 degrees. Roast an additional 30 to 40 minutes. This is a foolproof method for rare roast beef.

If you prefer medium or well done roast beef, then add 15 to 20 minutes to this Step II.

Do not open oven door from time you place roast in oven until you are ready to serve the roast. A suggestion; remove roast 15 minutes before dinner is served, then the juices of the roast will be absorbed, giving you an even better roast.

★Slumgullion — from one end of the beef scale to the other. This time, the recipe uses stew beef. It comes from the long time friend who has contributed many recipes to my Cooking Down East column. I will say this is one of the most popular recipes I have ever used. As you read the recipe you will learn why it has such great appeal.

SLUMGULLION

2 pounds stew beef
4 onions
1 large can tomatoes; if
  home canned, 1 quart

1 teaspoon poultry
  seasoning
Salt to taste

Cut stew beef into about 1-inch cubes. Do not brown. Place in a 2-quart casserole. Cover with sliced onions. Salt the onions. Turn canned tomatoes over onions, add another sprinkle of salt and the 1 teaspoon poultry seasoning.

Cover pan; use foil if no cover available. Bake at 275 or 300 degrees for about 3 hours. In meantime, combine 1/3 cup flour with 1/2 cup cold water, mix and allow to stand — this prevents lumping when stirred into hot beef mixture. When meat is tender, stir in the flour mixture; this thickens the slumgullion immediately. Serves 6 to 8. Freezes well. Use a double boiler to thaw and reheat.

Serve with mashed potatoes or on cooked noodles.

BAKED HAMBURG

1½ pounds hamburg
2 cups toasted bread
  crumbs
1 cup milk
1 egg, beaten
1 slice onion, minced

1 teaspoon salt
¼ teaspoon pepper
¼ teaspoon nutmeg
1 teaspoon lemon juice

Butter a shallow pan, about 7 x 11 inches, preferably one that may be brought to the table for serving.

Toast enough slices of bread to make 2 cups crumbs. When cool, put toast through grinder, soak crumbs in the milk for 1 hour. Add beaten egg and remaining ingredients. You will be pleased at the good flavor the lemon juice and nutmeg give to the meat.

Turn mixture lightly into the greased pan, allow to stand about 1 hour before baking. If you wish, you can mix and place pan in refrigerator overnight before baking. This is not necessary but it sometimes is helpful. Bake at 350 degrees for 1¼ hours.

If you have fresh parsley, mince and sprinkle some on top of meat after removing from oven. Serve in squares at table. It is delicious topped with this mushroom sauce. Or you may prefer a tomato sauce.

MUSHROOM SAUCE

½ stick margarine, melted
¼ to ½ pound fresh
  mushrooms
2 to 4 tablespoons flour
1 tablespoon minced
  parsley

Salt, pepper to taste
1 tablespoon lemon juice
1½ cups water or light
  cream or evaporated
  skimmed milk

Melt margarine in frypan. Depending on size of family, use ¼ to ½ pound fresh mushrooms. They are not peeled, just washed and the tip of stems cut off. Slice thin through mushrooms, so cap and stem are together. Cook about 5 minutes in melted margarine. Sprinkle flour over mushrooms, stir lightly, using a low heat for all of this. Add seasonings, gently stir in water, cream or evaporated milk. Stir until thickened. Serve hot. Serves 8.

★Boiling beef is a long ago custom among Maine cooks. Very likely you still boil beef or you would like to learn. For a long time after we were married my husband occasionally asked, "Could we have some boiled beef?" You see, his mother cooked a pot roast in this way, with no browning, maybe using a pint or so of water and seasoning. Along toward the last of the cooking she added vegetables. It was a delicious dinner, almost like a boiled dinner; only this was not corned beef, but fresh pot roast beef.

Along came a day when I talked with my Gardiner friend, who suggested boiling fresh brisket. This is such a delicious dinner, all cooked in the same kettle. This is not a rolled brisket of beef, it is left flat. Just ask for fresh brisket of beef at your meat department.

BOILED FRESH BRISKET OF BEEF

Wipe fresh brisket of beef, leave flat and place in kettle. Add 1 cup water, 1 cup tomato juice, salt and pepper, a bay leaf and a slice of onion to kettle. Cover and bring to steaming point. Lower heat and allow to boil gently for 3 to 4 hours, depending upon amount of brisket. About 1 hour before serving, place pared potatoes and pared whole carrots in the liquor around the beef. Bring back to steaming point, reduce the heat and cook about 1 hour longer or until vegetables are tender. Onions may be added, if you wish.

Slice beef, arrange on platter and surround with vegetables, which naturally take on a delightful color from the tomato juice.

TO CORN FRESH BRISKET OF BEEF

Place fresh brisket of beef in a large bowl, so that cold water may be added to cover. Place a washed unpared raw potato in the water or use an uncooked egg. Start adding table salt and continue to add it to the water in the bowl until the potato or egg floats. Place the bowl in the refrigerator for 48 to 72 hours depending upon how corned you like your beef.

★This recipe is referred to as "the most used casserole in Unity," and that is the kind of recipe we like. The amount yields two good sized casseroles, one for giving and one for home use; or you could freeze one, if you liked.

UNITY BEEF CASSEROLE

1½ pounds ground beef
1 medium onion, diced
2 cans cream of mushroom soup
1½ cups milk

½ pound package medium noodles, cooked
½ pound American cheese, shredded
Buttered crumbs

Cook onion in about 3 tablespoons margarine. Add ground beef and cook until brown. Mix soup and milk together and add to meat. Cook and drain noodles, then add. Add shredded cheese and mix well.

Turn into 2 buttered casseroles. Top with buttered crumbs. Bake ½ hour at 350 degrees.

★The ways in which we may use ground beef seem endless and we are constantly looking for different uses. This recipe has the addition of thin slices of ham, also cheese to make it very special — the kind you will want to serve to guests. It came our way from Houlton. As you can see, our recipes have come from many parts of Maine, making this a friend-ly cookbook.

COMPANY MEAT LOAF

2 eggs, beaten
¾ cup bread crumbs
½ cup tomato juice or sauce
½ teaspoon oregano leaves
½ teaspoon salt
2 tablespoons minced parsley

¼ teaspoon pepper
1 clove garlic, minced
2 pounds ground chuck
8 thin slices ham
6 ounces shredded mozzarella cheese
3 slices mozzarella cheese

Mix first nine ingredients together. Lay a piece of foil on counter. Pat mixture into 10 x 12-inch rectangle on foil. Arrange ham on meat. Sprinkle cheese on ham. Roll like a jelly roll. Place in 9 x 13-inch pan; leave on foil in pan, if you wish. Bake at 350 degrees for 1¼ hours. Place 3 slices mozzarella cheese on top of loaf, long enough for it to melt. Serves 8.

BAKED STUFFED GREEN PEPPERS

1 pound ground beef
1½ cups packaged stuffing
1½ cups milk

1 egg, beaten
½ teaspoon salt
4 large or 6 medium green peppers

Combine dry packaged stuffing, milk, beaten egg and salt. Let stand 15 minutes or so, to let stuffing soak up the milk and egg. An egg in any meat loaf filling, you know, binds the ingredients together. In this recipe if you prefer, use your own ground bread crumbs. When 15 minutes is up, combine with ground beef. Use as a filling in green peppers prepared in the following manner.

TO PREPARE GREEN PEPPERS

Cut tops off peppers, remove seeds, wash and place in one inch cold water in covered saucepan. Bring to steaming point, lower heat and parboil peppers for 8 to 10 minutes. Remove to casserole, salt inside of peppers, fill with meat loaf filling. Bake at 400 degrees for 1 hour. Potatoes may be baked at the same temperature and time.

SKILLET HAMBURG RICE

2 small onions
1 pound ground chuck
1 cup sliced celery
1 small can mushrooms
  and juice

1 cup raw rice
1 can consomme
½ cup water

Use small amount of fat, melt in frypan, add onions that have been sliced. Add ground chuck and cook slowly until brown. Add celery and mushrooms and allow to simmer. Add consomme and water.

Place raw rice in sieve and run cold water through it, so it is washed thoroughly. Stir rice into mixture. Cover skillet or frypan, using foil if pan has no cover; simmer about ½ hour or until rice is done. This amount serves 4, generously.

HAMBURG-NOODLE
CASSEROLE

8-ounce package medium
  noodles, 4 cups,
  uncooked
1 tablespoon margarine
1 pound hamburg
2 eight-ounce cans
  tomato sauce
1 tablespoon minced
  green pepper

½ pound cottage cheese,
  large curd
One 8-ounce package
  cream cheese
¼ cup dairy sour cream
1/3 cup snipped chives or
  finely minced onion
2 tablespoons melted butter
  or margarine

Cook noodles and drain. Cook meat in 1 tablespoon margarine. Stir in tomato sauce. Combine cheeses, sour cream, green pepper and chives or onions. Using a buttered

2-quart casserole, spread ½ the cooked noodles. Cover with the mixture of cheeses, then the remainder of noodles. Over this, dribble the melted butter. Turn the meat and tomato sauce over all. Refrigerate. When ready to cook, bring to room temperature, then bake at 375 degrees for 45 minutes. Serves 6.

★It was not too many years ago that this method of preparing a pot roast was sweeping the country and the recipe swept into Maine. Actually, that was the name of the recipe — Sweep Steak. We are more apt to call it easy pot roast, for that is exactly what it is.

EASY POT ROAST

**2 to 3 pounds beef for
  pot roast
Package onion soup mix**

**Can undiluted cream of
  mushroom soup
Heavy aluminum foil**

Place beef on piece heavy aluminum foil in a baking pan. Sprinkle dry onion soup mix over the beef, turn cream of mushroom soup over top. Seal the foil snugly. This is placed in the pan in case it should run out. Bake at 300 degrees for 3 hours. If you wanted this to cook all day, you could use 200 degrees for 8 hours. Naturally, when you unwrap the package, you will have a perfectly delicious gravy all ready for serving. No seasonings needed, of course.

★Every so often a recipe comes along that is great fun. It is that way with the following. If you should put beef, potatoes and carrots into a covered casserole, place that on a rack in a kettle, with about 1 quart water in the kettle, then place a cover on the kettle, you would have "Meat In A Closed Pot." Of course you would, and that is the name of this recipe. It is so easy to do and delicious to eat. With it you will serve stewed tomatoes.

MEAT IN CLOSED POT

**1½ pounds stew beef
6 pared potatoes**

**6 pared carrots
Onions, if you wish**

Cut stew beef or beef of your choice into 1-inch cubes. This beef is not browned, merely placed in bottom of casserole. Slice the pared potatoes over beef, slice carrots over the potato, the same with onions. Dot top of vegetables with butter or margarine. No seasoning needed and no water is used in the casserole. This makes its own juice and the natural flavors provide the seasoning.

Cover this casserole, using foil if the casserole has no cover. Use kettle large enough for a rack placed in bottom. Use 1 quart water in kettle, place casserole on rack, cover kettle. Bring to steaming point, lower heat and boil slowly for 4 hours.

When time is up, remove casserole to table for serving. It's as easy as that. Serve spoonfuls onto dinner plates, spooning some of the dip over all. Stewed tomatoes are just the thing to serve with this. A salad would be good, too.

★Barbecued Steak Strips to be served on rice is another recipe to be cooked on top of the stove or in your electric frypan. A recipe that is real company fare.

BARBECUED STEAK STRIPS

1 pound top of round steak	½ teaspoon chili powder
1 tablespoon oil	1 teaspoon Worcestershire
½ cup catsup	sauce
1 teaspoon dry mustard	1 tablespoon minced onion
1 clove garlic	½ cup Burgundy wine

Cut beef in thin strips. Heat oil in frypan, cook onion slowly. Add whole clove garlic, peeled; then it may be removed after cooking in oil to give flavor. Or you may mince garlic and leave in sauce. Lay steak strips in oil and brown lightly; add remaining ingredients. Usually I add ½ cup water so there will be more sauce. Cover pan, cook slowly for at least an hour until steak strips are tender. If sauce thickens too much, add more water while continuing the cooking. Serve on rice.

★Perhaps you have never cooked lamb shanks. Have you ever eaten them? You really have a treat in store, both in the cooking and in the eating. Do you live alone? Are there just two in your family? Longing for a roast leg of lamb? Then, lamb shanks is the answer. They are the answer if your family is larger, too. Or if you are expecting guests. There is just nothing like lamb shanks. A shank is the lower part of the leg of lamb, so there needs to be water used in the cooking. The cooking needs to be low and slow. You will find this a favorite dinner.

BRAISED LAMB SHANKS

Allow one lamb shank per serving. Sometimes they have more meat on them and a half shank would be all you could possibly eat. Wipe the shanks, put flour, salt and pepper into a paper bag, and shake up the shanks in this mixture.

Brown shanks in melted margarine in frypan. If you wish, you may cook them right in the frypan, or you may use an electric frypan. You will probably agree with me that the oven is the very best place for cooking them.

Place browned shanks in a casserole. Pour 1 cup water into frypan, bring to boil, stir up mixture, pour over shanks. Cover pan, bake at 300 degrees for about 2½ hours. If it suits you better to use 275 degrees, then allow about 3 to 3½ hours.

If you decide to cook them in a covered pan on top of stove, use 1 cup water, place cover on pan, bring to steam, lower heat and cook slowly for 2 to 2½ hours.

Place shanks on platter, spoon the "dip" over them. If you have baked them in a casserole, remove cover and place on table for serving.

Rice is very good served with the lamb shanks. If you are using your oven, then use a smaller covered casserole, twice as much water as rice, add salt, place cover on casserole and bake about 1½ hours at 300 degrees. Rice will be ready for serving, just as it comes from the oven. Add piece of butter and pepper to this if you want, for seasoning, but you will find the lamb dip has delicious flavor.

★Baked hot dogs will be good any time of year. If it is cold weather, you may want to serve them with scalloped potatoes. If you serve them during the summer months, then potato salad will be a good accompaniment.

BAKED HOT DOGS

1 small onion, diced	1 teaspoon paprika
2 tablespoons margarine	½ cup catsup
Dash of black pepper	¼ cup vinegar
2 tablespoons sugar	¾ cup water
1 teaspoon dry mustard	

Saute onion in margarine until soft. Add remaining ingredients, bring to a boil. Boil slowly for 2 or 3 minutes. Allow 2 hot dogs per person. Split them and place in shallow baking pan. Pour sauce over hot dogs, bake at 350 degrees for 30 minutes. This is enough sauce for 12 hot dogs.

TO COOK LINK SAUSAGES THE OLD-FASHIONED WAY

Get out your heavy old black spider. Separate link sausages and place in pan. Pour water into pan so it comes just up over the sausages. Bring water to boiling point and continue to boil until water cooks away, lower heat and gently turn sausages until they are golden brown. This is an excellent way of making certain sausage meat is well-cooked, if you decide to cook the sausages on top of the stove.

BAKED CANADIAN BACON

Use a whole Canadian Bacon, which will probably weigh 2 to 3 pounds. Place in baking pan, fat side up. Pour ½ cup beer over whole bacon. Bake at 325 degrees, 45 minutes, basting occasionally. If you wish, use cider or gingerale.

Mix ¾ cup brown sugar with ½ teaspoon dry mustard and enough beer to make a paste. Spread on bacon. Bake one hour longer. Baste occasionally. Serve, sliced very thin. This is good for a party; with it serve thin party rye bread.

BAKED HAM SLICES

Place thick slice of ham in large pan that can be covered. If pan you are using has no cover, use foil. Stick several whole cloves in fat around edges. Better score (cut with sharp knife) edges, too, then they will not curl up. Drain juice from a small can sliced pineapple, mix with 1 cup gingerale, add ½ cup brown sugar. Mix and pour over ham slice. Secure slices of pineapple to ham, using toothpicks. Cover pan of ham. Bake at 350 degrees for 1½ hours.

A thick slice of ham baked in 1 cup milk and ½ cup gingerale for about 1 hour at 325 degrees is good, too.

SCALLOPED HAM AND POTATOES

5 cups thinly sliced, pared raw potatoes
3 cups diced, cooked ham

1 cup thinly sliced onions
3 cups thin white sauce

Arrange potatoes, ham and onion in alternate layers in casserole. Pour the white sauce over all, cover and bake at 375 degrees for one hour. Remove cover and bake 30 minutes longer or until potatoes are tender. Serves 6.

THIN WHITE SAUCE

3 tablespoons margarine
3 tablespoons flour
Dash of black pepper

1½ teaspoons salt
3 cups milk

Melt margarine over a low heat. Stir in flour, salt and pepper. Add milk gradually, continue to stir and cook over a low heat until sauce thickens.

HAM AND VEAL LOAF

1 pound veal, ground
1 pound ham, ground
2 cups soft bread crumbs
1½ cups milk

½ teaspoon pepper
1 teaspoon celery salt
1 egg, beaten

This recipe which came to me from my next door neighbor is simple to make, has a delicious flavor and is sure to be popular in your family, too. It makes a large meat loaf, serves 8. You may want to make 2, bake them both and freeze one. There is no onion in the recipe, so you may want to add onion juice.

Make a dressing of bread crumbs, milk, pepper, celery salt and beaten egg. Combine with the 2 kinds of ground meat. Turn into large loaf pan that has been greased. It will fit into your 9 x 5 x 3-inch pan.

Bake at 375 degrees for 1 hour to 1¼ hours. You will find this is good served cold, too. It also makes excellent sandwiches.

★Mustard sauce served on hot ham loaf is often an added attraction. It too is served hot but may be prepared ahead and stored in the refrigerator, then reheated in top of the double boiler.

MUSTARD SAUCE

2 eggs, beaten
1 cup tomato soup,
  undiluted
½ cup prepared mustard
1 cup sugar
1 cup vinegar
1 stick margarine

Cook all together in top of double boiler until thick. Place margarine in top of double boiler, allowing it to melt, while you beat the eggs and combine with other ingredients; then start stirring all ingredients together over hot water, until thickened. Serve hot. To store, keep in covered jar in refrigerator.

CORNED BEEF CASSEROLE

8-ounce package macaroni
  or noodles
12-ounce can corned beef
¼ pound American cheese,
  cut up
1 can cream of chicken or
  cream of mushroom soup
1 cup milk
½ cup minced onion
Buttered crumbs for
  topping

Cook macaroni or noodles and drain. Cut up corned beef and cheese. Mix soup with milk. Combine all ingredients, leaving onion raw. Turn into buttered 2-quart casserole. Top with buttered crumbs. Bake one hour at 350 degrees.

★This really isn't a stew at all but you will like its name and the ease with which you may prepare it.

ONE-TWO-THREE STEW

1 package dehydrated
  onion soup mix
2 cans cream of mushroom
  soup, plus ½ cup water

3 pounds lean stew
  beef, cut in cubes

Combine all ingredients, cutting down on amount of dry onion soup mix if you like. Turn into large, buttered casserole. Cover. Bake for 3 hours at 300 degrees or 4 hours at 250 degrees. This amount serves 8.

Eggs and Cheese

The critical period in matrimony is breakfast time

CHAPTER FIVE

Eggs and Cheese

There is an enchantment in the age-old question, "Which came first, the chicken or the egg?" Maine chicken came first in this cookbook, but it is equally important to talk about Maine eggs.

Yet, it is only right we entitle this chapter Eggs and Cheese, for they have been going around together for years. You will find recipes using eggs and recipes using cheese and more often than not there are recipes using both.

We could never consume all the eggs that are produced in Maine. A large proportion of Maine eggs are shipped out of state.

Eggs are man's most nutritious food. Did you ever think they are designed by nature to supply all the nutrients needed in the development of a healthy, sturdy chick? Except for the shell, there is no waste — the egg meat is fully and easily digested. If you wanted to, you could eat the shell — it is an excellent source of calcium.

Learning about eggs and their nutritive value makes us more aware of what has always been meant when people say, "He's a good egg."

It's no wonder that a meal including eggs gives you a satisfactory feeling and you like knowing it is one that really sticks with you, without thinking you are all loaded down with calories.

We talk a lot about convenience foods. It's easy to think that eggs fall into this category; but so does cheese. It is one of the most versatile and most nutritious of foods, so it is used frequently by homemakers in meal planning and food preparation.

Many questions are asked about cooking cheese, and most important of all is remembering to keep the heat low.

Cheese needs just enough heat to melt and blend with other ingredients. High heat or long cooking makes cheese tough and stringy.

Add cheese to other ingredients in small pieces; it spreads more evenly and cooks in a shorter time. If it is a cheese sauce you are making, add the cheese just at the last minute and cook only until it melts.

If cheese is to be grated or shredded, the job is easier if you work with cold cheese taken directly from the refrigerator. Except for soft unripened cheese such as cottage cheese or cream cheese, all cheese tastes better if served at room temperature.

It is a must, however, that both eggs and cheese need to be kept refrigerated because they are protein foods.

★Everyone has to be new at making an omelet sometime and even though you may be quite professional at this in your own kitchen, chances are you would like a review.

BASIC OMELET
(Single Serving)

2 eggs	¼ teaspoon salt
2 teaspoons water	1 tablespoon butter or margarine

Mix eggs, water and salt with a fork until yolks and whites are blended. Meanwhile, heat butter or margarine in a pan or heavy skillet, preferably one with low, gently sloping sides. When butter is hot enough to sizzle a drop of water, pour in egg mixture. Mixture should bubble and begin to cook at outer edges.

With a pancake turner, slide the cooked egg toward the center of the pan and tilt pan so uncooked portion flows onto the surface. Do this all around the pan, shaking the pan back and forth periodically to keep mixture sliding freely.

When the mixture no longer flows and is moist and creamy on top, the omelet is ready to be folded over. However, if you have in mind adding some filling such as bits of cheddar cheese, crumbled cooked bacon, sauteed mushroom slices or precooked vegetables like asparagus, then this is the time to do it. At this point the entire surface of the pan should be covered with the egg mixture.

With pan handle toward you, place filling on the left half of the omelet. Slide the pancake turner under the right half and fold it over the left half.

Tilt pan so omelet slides to the left rim. Place the rim on the serving platter and slide the omelet until it extends onto the platter about one inch. Then turn the pan over.

FRENCH TOAST

2 eggs   ½ cup milk
½ teaspoon salt   6 slices bread

Use a shallow dish for preparing eggs and milk, like an old fashioned soup plate. These ingredients will give you an idea of proportions; use according to number of slices of French toast you need.

Using a fork, beat eggs slightly, add salt and milk, blend ingredients together. Dip each slice of bread into the mixture until well soaked. Cook on both sides in a skillet using margarine or oil. Make certain slices are cooked through as well as browned.

Making French toast for a crowd? Try it the easy oven way, adding one more egg and increasing the milk to one cup if you want 12 slices of French toast or enough to serve 6.

Dip bread slices into mixture, place on well-greased cookie sheet, brown in 450-degree oven for about 10 minutes. Turn toast, add more butter if needed, complete browning.

French toast is delicious served with syrup, but you have never eaten it at its best unless you have served it with chilled applesauce.

MAINE APPLESAUCE

The number of apples you use is determined by the amount of sauce you want to make. Three quarts of cut-up apples will make about 1½ quarts of strained applesauce.

Wash the apples, quarter them, cut out the blossom and stem end and any blemishes. Do not pare or core. Put apples in saucepan, add about 1 cup water and a sprinkle of salt. Cover pan, bring to steaming point; lower heat, cook about 15 minutes or until apples are soft.

Use wooden spoon, press apples through a sieve. Keep on pressing until you have every bit of goodness from the fruit or use a food mill for this.

Add ½ to 1 cup granulated sugar, a shake of nutmeg and a shake of cinnamon. Serve hot or cold. On French toast it is best to serve cold applesauce spooned over the hot slices of toast. If you have extra sauce, turn into a plastic container, cool it, cover and place in freezer. It will keep for months.

BAKED EGG CUPS

Cut crusts from as many slices of bread as you will need. Brush with melted butter or margarine. Press each slice gently into a well-greased muffin cup. Bake about 7 minutes at 350 degrees

Break an egg into a cup, then slide into center of each slice of toasted bread. Season with salt and pepper. Sprinkle eggs with parmesan cheese, if desired. Place pan back in oven. Bake about 10 minutes at 350 degrees.

★Egg pancake could become a favorite breakfast, but it will be just as good for lunch or supper. It looks like a glorified popover. This recipe did not come from our family, but it is an old-fashioned recipe and came from down along the New Meadows River, too.

EGG PANCAKE

2 eggs, well beaten	1/3 cup sifted flour
½ cup milk	¼ teaspoon salt

Beat ingredients together in order given. Heat a 9-inch skillet, using 2 tablespoons shortening. If you have a heavy black spider, do use it, for you are going to slide this egg pancake into the oven shortly.

Pour batter into skillet. Allow to cook on top of stove for a minute or two. Then place pan in 425 degree oven and bake from 15 to 25 minutes until "popped" and golden brown. Keep in mind, a heavy black frypan absorbs heat faster and egg pancake will cook more quickly in it. The length of time will depend on kind of pan used. Remember too, some pans cannot go into the oven because of their handle.

Serve hot with pats of butter or crispy bacon.

★If you like grilled cheese sandwiches, you should try one by the ironing method. It is a slick trick. After using this recipe in my column I was amazed that office secretaries went off to work tugging their electric irons, so they might enjoy a hot sandwich at noon.

IRONED GRILLED CHEESE SANDWICH

Make a cheese sandwich. You do not need to butter the outside of the sandwich. Wrap a piece of aluminum foil around it — just one thickness of foil; do not overlap it. Place electric iron on it — using highest heat. Peek inside foil to make sure the bread is toasted brown. Turn sandwich and iron the other side until golden brown. The cheese melts and in minutes you have an easily prepared and delicious grilled cheese sandwich.

DEVILED EGGS

8 hard-cooked eggs
2½ teaspoons lemon juice
  or pickle juice
1 teaspoon prepared
  mustard
1 teaspoon Worcestershire
  sauce

½ teaspoon salt
Few grains pepper
½ teaspoon minced onion
3 tablespoons mayonnaise

Hard cook the eggs; peel and cut the eggs in half, lengthwise. Mash the yellow and add rest of ingredients. Refill egg whites. Chill and serve.

★People speak about store cheese, rat cheese and mouse-trap cheese. Actually, they are referring to aged cheddar cheese. This sandwich filling recipe came from Camden and it was recommended that store cheese be used. The seasonings can be adapted to suit the tastes of your family. This is a hearty sandwich and I like its name.

FRIDAY SANDWICH FILLING

3 hard cooked eggs
1 cup cut-up store cheese
1 small green pepper,
   washed, seeds removed,
   cut into pieces

Salad dressing or
   mayonnaise to mix
1 teaspoon horse-radish
Salt to taste

These ingredients may all be put through a food grinder, using a coarse blade. Or in the good old Maine way, you could get out your wooden bowl and chopping knife and chop these ingredients fine. After chopping or grinding, add the mayonnaise, horse-radish and salt, seasoning to suit your family's taste.

★Your electric frypan or a covered skillet used on top of your stove will provide you a hearty dinner in about 35 minutes time. It is good to try macaroni and cheese in a different way and the seasonings you add will give a delicious flavor. Of course, you may always leave out any seasonings that do not appeal to you.

SKILLET MACARONI AND CHEESE

1 stick margarine
¼ cup minced onion
½ cup chopped green
   pepper
1 teaspoon salt
¼ teaspoon pepper
¼ teaspoon dry mustard
¼ teaspoon oregano

One 8-ounce package
   elbow macaroni
2 cups water
1 tablespoon flour
One 13-ounce can
   evaporated milk
2 tablespoons chopped
   pimiento
2 cups cheddar cheese,
   finely chopped

Melt margarine in electric frypan or skillet on range. Add onion and green pepper; cook until tender, using low heat. Stir in salt, pepper, mustard and oregano. Add macaroni and water, turn up temperature or heat. Bring to a boil, stir so it is well mixed. Cover and simmer in electric frypan at 220 degrees or on low heat on top of range. Make certain the macaroni is cooked to your liking before adding rest of ingredients.

Sprinkle flour over all, blend well. Stir in evaporated milk. Cook another 5 minutes on a low heat. Add pimiento and cut-up cheese; heat, stirring occasionally, until cheese has melted. Serves 6 to 8.

CHEESE SANDWICH CASSEROLE

3 eggs, beaten
2 cups milk
Salt and pepper
Bit of Worcestershire
 sauce

Using sharp cheddar
cheese, make 5 or 6
sandwiches

Use a low casserole about 7 x 11 inches. Butter it. Place the sandwiches in casserole. Beat eggs, add milk and seasonings, pour over sandwiches. Vary these sandwich fillings, adding a slice of ham or chopped ham sometimes.

The beauty of making this casserole is that once it is assembled, it has to stand for at least an hour before baking and 2 hours is better. How about this? Allow it to stand all day, refrigerated; or, if it suits you better, then overnight. Bring to room temperature, then bake at 350 degrees for 45 minutes.

You could call this recipe a "let yourself go" one, and as long as you have decided to do this, why not lay tomato slices or tomato halves on top for the last 10 minutes.

★Cheese crunchies will be a good addition to any party, plus the fact you may mix them, chill them, then bake them to be served hot from your oven. Or you could chill the dough, bake them and freeze the baked crunchies; then they will only need to be warmed for serving. Actually, you do not need to serve them warm anyway, they are delicious just as you take them out of the cookie jar.

CHEESE CRUNCHIES

2 cups grated sharp cheese   2 cups sifted flour
2 sticks margarine, at room   Dash of red pepper
   temperature   ½ teaspoon onion salt
2 cups rice crispies

You notice there are no eggs, which is correct. The first time I made these I grated the cheese, which is not necessary. Buy it all grated. Mix all ingredients together, chill dough. Form into balls and flatten on ungreased cookie sheet. Bake at 400 degrees for about 10 minutes.

★You can hardly go wrong about cooking an egg. There is one thing you have to keep in mind — eggs have to be cooked at low to moderate temperature. It is common knowledge that high temperatures toughen eggs. You learn from experience that when a custard sauce curdles (which you may correct when sauce is cold by using an egg beater) too high a temperature or too long cooking was involved. The same is true when a custard pie "wheys".

Nothing encourages the use of eggs like a new recipe or an old one. It was a number of years ago that I wrote a story about Maine eggs, with pictures. The one I like best is that of the son of friends in Rockland. Now, with his own family, I'm sure Jon cherishes this picture, too. He had just become an Eagle Scout and the caption reads, "Any Boy Scout can cook his own meal as long as he's making a toad-in-the-hole." Come to think of it, he was a good kid to go along with this story. This is an old-fashioned recipe and you can hardly go wrong with it.

TOAD-IN-THE-HOLE

Cut a circle out of the center of a slice of bread, using a biscuit cutter. Fry bread in 3 tablespoons butter or margarine until crisp and brown on one side. Turn it over and break an egg in the circle. Better to break an egg into a cup, then slide it into the circle. Fry over low heat about 5 minutes or until egg is cooked. Season with salt and pepper.

★Shirring eggs is another oldtime means of cooking them in a simple way, and so good that you wonder why you do not do this more often. Especially when you think of the good food value of eggs.

SHIRRED EGGS

Use custard cups or ramekins, greased or oiled. Place 1 tablespoon cream in each. Carefully break an egg in each, sprinkle with salt and pepper, arrange in a shallow pan, bake at 350 degrees for 15 to 20 minutes or until eggs are set.

Another method of doing shirred eggs is to grease the custard cups or ramekins and line them with buttered bread crumbs. Carefully break an egg in each, sprinkle with salt and pepper, cover each with 1 tablespoon cream or milk. Arrange in a shallow pan, bake at 350 degrees for 15 to 20 minutes or until eggs are set.

★The next two recipes are from Machias and this is where they really cook Down East. I like remembering eating good foods using eggs and cheese, seated at tables in cozy, warm kitchens. It was so typically Maine in both instances.

EASY CHEESE SOUFFLE

6 eggs, separated   **1 can cheese soup, heated**

Beat whites and yolks, separately. Heat cheese soup, stir soup into beaten egg yolks. Fold in the beaten egg whites. Turn into ungreased two-quart casserole. Place casserole in shallow pan containing water. Bake at 300 degrees for $1\frac{1}{4}$ hours or at 400 degrees for 30 minutes (either way works well). There is no seasoning added to this souffle, for the cheese soup is used undiluted. Serves 4, generously.

Variation: Use 1 can cream of asparagus soup and 1 cup shredded sharp cheese, heated together in place of can of cheese soup.

As with all cheese souffles, it needs to be served immediately.

CHEESE TOPPING FOR CRACKERS

One can (4 oz.) grated American cheese	Dash of Tabasco sauce
1 stick margarine	1 teaspoon prepared mustard
Dash of Worcestershire sauce	Your favorite kind of crackers

Cream margarine, blend in grated cheese and add seasonings. Spread on your favorite kind of crackers. Sprinkle with paprika. Bake slowly at 250 degrees. Serve hot or cold.

★Economically, eggs fit well into meal planning. Casseroles using eggs are popular and these next 3 recipes will be liked by your family and guests alike.

GOLDEN STUFFED EGG CASSEROLE

Make necessary number of stuffed eggs. This recipe is for six shelled hard cooked eggs. Cut in half lengthwise; remove yolks, lay whites aside. Mash yolks using a fork and add:

¼ teaspoon salt	Enough mayonnaise to mix
Dash of pepper	Few drops onion juice
¼ teaspoon dry mustard	

Refill whites with this mixture, rounding the filling. Make following sauce and spoon over stuffed eggs that have been placed in a shallow casserole:

1 can golden mushroom soup	Add pinch of curry powder to liquid from can of mushrooms
1 can cream of mushroom soup	
1 small can mushrooms, stems and pieces	

Mix soups, mushrooms and liquid together. This sauce is not cooked nor heated. Spoon over eggs. Bake at 325 degrees for 25 minutes. Sprinkle top with toasted flaked cocoanut mixed with a few chopped nuts. Or buttered crumbs may be sprinkled on top if you would prefer that for topping. Serves 4 to 6.

★This is another Aroostook County recipe. You will like everything about it, including the fact this is uncooked macaroni mixed with the ingredients. All the ingredients are mixed together, turned into the casserole, refrigerated for 8 to 24 hours, then baked.

MACARONI CASSEROLE

2 cups uncooked elbow macaroni

2 cans cream of mushroom soup

4 ounces dried beef — less than this may be used

1½ cups cheddar cheese, cubed

4 hard-cooked eggs, diced

¼ cup minced onion

2 cups milk

No seasoning needed

Combine all ingredients, turn into 2-quart casserole. Cover and refrigerate overnight or for at least 8 hours. This, of course, allows the uncooked macaroni to soften before baking.

Bring to room temperature and bake uncovered at 350 degrees for one hour. Serves 6, generously.

COMPANY TUNA BAKE

1 cup elbow macaroni

One 3-ounce package cream cheese, softened

1 can cream of mushroom soup, undiluted

One 7-ounce can tuna, drained and flaked

1 tablespoon chopped pimiento

1 tablespoon chopped onion

1 teaspoon prepared mustard

1/3 cup milk

½ cup bread crumbs

2 tablespoons margarine, melted

Cook macaroni and drain. Using mixer, blend cream cheese and mushroom soup until smooth. Stir in tuna, pimiento, onion, mustard, milk and cooked macaroni. Turn into buttered 1½-quart casserole. Mix crumbs with melted margarine, sprinkle evenly over tuna mixture. Bake at 375 degrees about 25 minutes. Serves 4.

★You could not find a better use for eggs than using them in a sunshine cake, especially if a dessert is what you have in mind. This is an old-fashioned recipe, yet very much in demand these days.

SUNSHINE CAKE

6 eggs separated 1 teaspoon cream of tartar
1 cup sugar ¼ teaspoon salt
1 cup sifted flour 1 teaspoon vanilla

Separate eggs. Beat whites until stiff, add salt, then beat in one-half of the sugar. Add vanilla.

Beat egg yolks until thick and light-colored, add remaining sugar. Fold together with beaten egg whites.

Sift flour with cream of tartar. Fold into combined egg mixture. Turn into large size ungreased angel cake pan. Bake at 325 degrees for 45 minutes. Test for doneness.

Vegetables

*Viva vital, vigorous, venerable, veritable,
versatile, vitamin-rich vegetables!*

CHAPTER SIX

Vegetables

An entire book could be written about public baked bean suppers in Maine. This age-old way of raising money for church and organizations has been going on for generations.

Most Maine cooks at one time or another have been involved in putting on a baked bean supper. There are other kinds of public suppers. A harvest supper held in the fall is another way of showing off Maine vegetables. Of course there is always pumpkin pie for dessert.

When we talk about public suppers, we do not forget chicken pie suppers, for they, too, are a heritage money-raiser. Down East they put on dried fish suppers, with pork scraps, boiled potatoes, pickled beets and mashed turnip. And pie.

Besides all the work involved, whether it is church, grange, American Legion, fraternal order or all the other organizations that need to raise money, there is the to-getherness that is important.

And the humor. My father joked with my mother about the food she cooked, the work she did in serving the supper, the dishes to wash, then he had to pay for the food we ate. But every father does that, even today. For public suppers are as popular as ever. Sometimes I feel they are even more so.

A poster in a store window, a placard on a bulletin board, an advertisement in a newspaper, an announcement on the radio that there is going to be a Saturday night supper to benefit an organization and people line up to buy their tickets. Early, too, for a 5 o'clock suppertime may find people already seated at tables by 4:30. They could have driven several miles to get to the place where the baked bean supper is being held.

No, it would not be any fun at all if organizations decided each member could contribute a certain sum and the public supper would be done away with.

A Maine cook has something else in mind as she bakes the beans, makes her jellied salad or a favorite casserole, frosts her cake. She is showing off her ability as a cook. She has reason to; her mother did it before her and she takes pride in the fact that her husband remarks to his waitress, "Could you see if I could have a piece of my wife's cake — it's that white cake down there at the other end of the table. The one with the chocolate frosting."

Yes, it is traditional to put on public suppers all over Maine, just as other parts of the country do, to raise money for groups. Everywhere they are well attended, for people know they are getting something special for their money.

★Maine baked beans mean just one thing — it is Saturday night. Whether you bake them for your own family or to be shared, it is our traditional Saturday night supper.

MAINE BAKED BEANS

1 pound dry beans (about 2 cups)	½ teaspoon dry mustard
2 tablespoons granulated sugar	2 tablespoons molasses
1 teaspoon salt	½ pound salt pork
Few grains black pepper	About 2½ cups boiling water

Pick over dry beans. Wash them. Place in a good sized bowl. Cover with cold water. Soak overnight. If you forget to soak them, then in the morning parboil them in water to cover, just until the skins wrinkle. If you soak them, you do not need to parboil them.

In the morning, drain beans. Place in a beanpot. Mix all seasonings together in a small bowl. Turn into beanpot on top of soaked, drained beans and mix together until all beans are coated with seasonings. Take care not to add too much molasses; it can cause beans to harden as they bake.

Add boiling water, about 2½ cups or enough to cover beans in the pot. Score salt pork by making gashes in it. Wash pork in hot water. Place it on top of the beans. Cover beanpot. Place in oven and bake at 250 degrees for 8 hours. They should not be stirred but they need attention occasionally, for they need to be kept covered with boiling water at all times.

Keep beanpot covered until the last hour of baking, then remove cover so beans will brown on top.

If you are longing for baked beans but salt pork is eliminated from your diet, then do exactly as above except omit the salt pork and use 4 tablespoons cooking oil per pound dry beans or 2 tablespoons cooking oil per cup of dry beans.

PARSNIPS

Parsnips are available in our markets nearly year round, and they are an easily prepared vegetable when done in this manner. Cut off ends, pare parsnips, wash, cut in half, then cut those pieces in half, unless they are very large parsnips — then you will cut each parsnip into more pieces. Place in saucepan with about one inch of water, add salt, cover pan, bring to steaming point; lower heat and cook about 10 minutes. Take care not to overcook them for they become mushy. Drain, return to saucepan, add butter, more salt if necessary, and pepper.

★If you have ever looked for the directions for cooking shell beans, then you will appreciate finding them here. It could be that in Maine we cook more shell beans than anywhere else. If we have making Maine succotash in mind, we have to cook the shell beans first.

TO COOK FRESH SHELL BEANS

Using about 1 cup cold water to 3 cups shelled beans, add salt, cover pan, bring to steaming point; lower heat and cook for at least 40 minutes or until tender. Hopefully, the water will be mostly absorbed. Take care they do not burn. Add milk or cream, salt, pepper and butter. Serve in sauce dishes.

TO MAKE MAINE SUCCOTASH

In some parts of the country, succotash is made by combining corn cut from the cob with lima beans. It just so happens that in Maine we combine cooked corn cut from the cob with cooked shell beans. Add cream or milk, a piece of butter, salt and pepper to taste.

Try combining a can of cream style corn with one can of shell beans in top of double boiler, add cream or milk, a piece of butter, salt and pepper. Serve in sauce dishes. This is a good vegetable to serve with meat loaf and baked potatoes.

★Whether you call them stewed beans or live in the north country and have always referred to them as Bean Swagin — pronounced Sway-gin — this favorite Maine food was popular with Maine lumberjacks. It was served with johnnycake. For generations cooks have handed down this way of preparing a food that "sticks to the ribs." There are oldtime cooks who would say, "Never fry the salt pork that is used, just put the pork and beans on to boil together." Either way, it is a delicious meal.

STEWED BEANS

Pick over one quart dry beans, wash and soak overnight. You will probably choose yellow eye beans, since they will be similar to the old fashioned beans of long ago. In the morning drain beans, put in kettle and cover with boilwater. Use one-half pound salt pork. This may be washed and placed in kettle or, as some cooks prefer, slice pork, then brown in frypan before adding to beans. Cover kettle, bring to steaming point; cook slowly for 4 to 5 hours or as you might hear a cook say, "Until they are all chowdered-up."

Stir occasionally. To keep from burning, you may need to add more water as they cook. Season with pepper before dishing up. If the pork does not season this enough, add salt. Either hot biscuits or big hot squares of johnnycake will be delicious with the stewed beans.

★This corn casserole, or corn pudding as it is sometimes called, was a favorite food when as "boarders" we gathered around the Burnham table in Bridgton, years ago. Mrs. Burnham cooked and served this in her heavy black spider. If you do not own one, then prepare in a frypan and turn mixture into a casserole for baking.

CORN CASSEROLE

2 tablespoons margarine	1 can cream style corn
1 small onion, diced	(2 cups)
4 tablespoons flour	2 eggs, beaten
2 cups milk	Buttered crumbs for
Salt and pepper to taste	topping

Melt margarine in frypan, dice onions, cook in melted fat until soft. Mix in flour, salt and pepper, add milk slowly, stirring and cooking over low heat until thickened. Add corn, mix well, remove from heat; add to beaten eggs, combine carefully, turn into buttered casserole. Top with buttered crumbs. Set casserole in pan with hot water. Bake at 350 degrees for 45 minutes. Serves 6.

★Corn Carney came to us from close-by Nova Scotia via two daughters who live in Hallowell. They suggest its use at the Easter season when ham is being served, but it is delicious as a supper dish. Notice it is mostly one cup measurements.

CORN CARNEY

1 cup cream style corn	1 egg, beaten
1 cup store cheese, cut fine	1 cup bread or cracker
1 cup milk	crumbs
Salt and pepper	Extra crumbs, buttered
	for topping

Butter a 1½ quart casserole. Mix all ingredients, turn into casserole, top with buttered crumbs. Place casserole in shallow pan of hot water. Bake at 350 degrees for 45 minutes.

TO COOK BEET GREENS

Prepare greens, scraping tiny beets with paring knife but leave small beets on greens. Wash well in several waters. You have learned that warm water cleans greens more easily than cold water. Place greens in kettle. Not more than ½ cup cold water will be needed, for water clings to the leaves. Add salt. Cover, bring to steaming point; lower heat and cook about 30 minutes or until tender. Remove to colander to drain. Use a knife and cut up greens and beets. Turn into serving dish. Add butter, salt and pepper. Stir to mix in seasonings.

BAKED ONION SLICES

6 large onions, peeled and sliced ½ inch thick	½ teaspoon butter
For each of these slices, you will need:	½ teaspoon brown sugar
	Dash of pepper
	Dash of seasoned salt

Place in a shallow pan. If your family is small use a pie plate. Bake uncovered in a 350 degree oven about 1 hour or until tender. Serves 4.

CANNED PEAS FRENCH-STYLE

One 17-ounce can peas	¼ teaspoon sugar
1 leaf of lettuce	Dash of pepper
¼ teaspoon salt	1 tablespoon butter, margarine or vegetable oil

Drain liquid from can of peas into saucepan. Place lettuce leaf in saucepan, add salt, sugar, pepper and butter; simmer about 10 minutes on low heat. Add peas and continue cooking on a low heat until thoroughly heated. Lettuce may or may not be removed. Serves 4.

What is so unusual about preparing canned peas in this way? It is a fine way of eliminating any canned taste.

★In case you are wondering how a recipe for a mock lobster sandwich got into a chapter on vegetables, I think you should hear a little story. A few years back, I used this recipe in my column, after having it in a file for a few years before that. I found it met with great enthusiasm. One woman wrote to tell me it is probably the very best recipe I have ever used in any column, so I could hardly leave it out of this cookbook, could I?

MOCK LOBSTER SANDWICH

2 slices bread
Spread one slice with
   deviled ham
Slice a smallish pared
   cucumber lengthwise
Place on deviled ham

On other slice of bread,
Place sliced, peeled tomato,
Dab mayonnaise on tomato
   slices
Put sandwich together
And enjoy!

EPICUREAN PEAS

Two 10-ounce packages
   frozen peas, cooked
   as directed
1 cup cream or milk
4 strips bacon
½ onion, minced
A bit of pepper

Small can mushrooms,
   stems and pieces
1 tablespoon flour
¼ cup sherry
1 tablespoon Worcester-
   shire sauce

Cut bacon and cook with onion in frypan for about 5 minutes. Stir in flour, add milk or cream, cook over low heat until slightly thickened. Add mushrooms and liquid, mixing well. Add remaining seasonings, adding salt if needed. Fold in the drained, cooked frozen peas. Serves 8. Peas cooked in this manner are company fare.

★This next recipe is another answer to, "What shall I serve for a vegetable to our guests?" This is so easy to concoct that you will like making it, as well as having broccoli in a way that will please your guests.

BROCCOLI FIXIN'S

2 packages frozen chopped broccoli	2 cups seasoned, packaged stuffing
1 can cream of celery soup, undiluted	1 stick margarine, melted

Cook frozen broccoli in covered pan in small amount of water for 3 minutes. Drain. Melt margarine, mix with dry packaged seasoned stuffing.

Butter a shallow 7 x 11-inch casserole. Spread layer of broccoli in bottom, then half the soup and half the buttered crumbs. Repeat. Bake at 350 degrees for 25 minutes. Serves 8.

★The introduction of summer squash many years ago to Maine people brought a whole new idea about squash cookery. Of course, it was a whole new kind of squash. In more recent years, Maine cooks have become acquainted with zucchini squash, equally delicious and as easy to cook as summer squash. After all, when you do not need to pare these two kinds of squashes, it makes for easier cooking.

We were accustomed to hard-shelled squash and not only can the paring be difficult, the cutting up can be, too. If you just happen to have a granite step by the back door, then you can wham the squash down on the step and watch it break into smaller pieces that you can cope with. If the shell is too hard for paring, then Maine cooks have the answer for that, too. They simply scoop out the seeds, wash it, place it in a shallow pan and bake it until tender. After that it is a simple matter to scoop out the cooked squash, mash it, season it and reheat it for serving.

It is best to choose summer squash or zucchini that has not grown too large, so the paring will cook up to be tender. If you grow your own, then you will have to share your squashes for nothing grows as fast as these two kinds of squash.

PAN-BROILED SUMMER SQUASH

Wash the summer squash, then slice—yes that is right, paring, seeds and all—into about 1-inch slices. Melt a piece of butter or margarine in a frying pan, season squash with salt and pepper and cook slowly over a medium heat until the slices are tender and a delicate brown. Serve on a platter.

FRIED ZUCCHINI SLICES

Use sufficient oil to cover surface of frypan. Prepare slices about a half hour ahead by slicing unpared squash in ¼-inch slices. Sprinkle with salt, spread on paper towel, allow to stand a half hour. This draws out the water from the squash so it may be fried without spattering. When drained, place in a paper bag with sufficient flour to coat. Beat one or two eggs, depending upon amount of squash you are frying, dip each piece of floured squash into egg, and fry in hot fat. Turn until lightly browned. Remove and drain on paper towel. Good hot or cold. Salt is only seasoning needed.

SMASHING SQUASH

2 pounds summer squash, sliced, cooked and drained

1 carrot, pared and grated

1 small onion, peeled and grated

1 stick margarine, melted and mixed with

One 8-ounce package herb stuffing, dry

Add ½ of the buttered stuffing to squash mixture

Add 1 cup dairy sour cream and 1 can cream of chicken soup, undiluted

Turn into shallow, buttered casserole

Top with remaining buttered stuffing

Bake at 350 degrees for 20 to 30 minutes. Serves 8.

STEAMED
SUMMER OR ZUCCHINI SQUASH

One way to cook summer squash or zucchini is to wash the squash, slice ½-inch thick, place in covered saucepan with small amount of water with a sprinkling of salt. Bring to steaming point, lower heat and cook 10 to 15 minutes. Test for doneness, drain, return to saucepan and place on a low heat to dry out, then mash, season with butter, salt and pepper. Add just a pinch of sugar, which improves nearly all vegetables.

ZUCCHINI WITH SWEET BASIL

1 tablespoon margarine
2 tablespoons olive oil
1 clove garlic, minced
1 small onion, diced
1 teaspoon basil, preferably
   fresh, minced
4 medium zucchini, washed
   cut in thin rounds

1 bay leaf
1 bouillon cube dissolved
   in 1 cup boiling water
1 whole peeled fresh
   tomato, cut up
Salt and pepper
Grated parmesan cheese
   for topping

Heat margarine and oil in large skillet, add garlic and onion and cook until lightly browned. Add bouillon cube dissolved in boiling water, the sliced unpared squash, basil and bay leaf. Stir to mix well. Add salt and pepper, cover, bring to steaming point and cook for 10 minutes. Remove cover, add cut-up, peeled tomato, stir in and finish cooking which takes only a few minutes. Turn into serving dish, sprinkle top with grated parmesan cheese. Serves 8.

The friend who gave me this recipe says this freezes well.

★In my great enthusiasm about summer squash and zucchini squash, a friend remarked to me, "I suppose you like eggplant, too!" She was right, and after you have made this scalloped eggplant you will, too.

SCALLOPED EGGPLANT

1 large eggplant, pared and
   diced (About 4 cups)
1/3 cup milk
1 can mushroom soup
1 egg, slightly beaten
¼ cup chopped onion
¾ cup packaged stuffing

Cheese Topping:
   ½ cup of the stuffing,
   mixed with 2 tablespoons
   melted margarine
1 cup shredded
   sharp cheese

Cook eggplant in small amount of salted water in covered saucepan for about 7 minutes. Drain. Stir in milk and soup. Blend in egg, add onion and 1/4 cup of stuffing. Toss lightly. Turn into buttered casserole. Sprinkle buttered crumbs over top of eggplant, then top with the cup of shredded cheese. Bake at 350 degrees for 20 to 30 minutes.

SPINACH CASSEROLE

2 or 3 packages frozen
  chopped spinach
1 pint dairy sour cream

1 package dried onion
  soup mix
Grated parmesan cheese

Combine dairy sour cream with as much of dry onion mix as you would like to use. In meantime, cook frozen spinach according to directions on package, drain and mix with cream mixture. Turn into buttered 7 x 11-inch casserole. Sprinkle grated cheese on top. Heat in moderate oven 325 to 350 degrees until it is bubbly. Two packages spinach serves 4 to 6. Three packages serves six to eight. Use same amount of cream and onion soup mix to either amount of frozen spinach.

CABBAGE WITH BACON SCALLOP

1 medium sized head of
  cabbage
6 slices bacon
2 tablespoons flour

3 tablespoons bacon fat
1 teaspoon salt or to taste
1/4 teaspoon pepper
2 cups cabbage broth

Shred cabbage, remove the hard core. Cook shredded cabbage in about 2 cups water in covered saucepan until cabbage is just tender. Drain and save this broth.

Cut bacon into 1-inch pieces and fry until crisp. Drain off all bacon fat but the 3 tablespoons called for in recipe. Blend the flour with fat, add salt and pepper, gradually add broth, stirring until a smooth gravy results.

Add this sauce and bacon pieces to cabbage and turn into greased casserole. Top with buttered crumb mixture (see next page). Bake at 375 degrees about 25 minutes or until it bubbles. Serves 6 to 8.

CRUMB TOPPING

3 tablespoons margarine,   2/3 cup seasoned bread
    melted   crumbs
½ cup grated parmesan cheese

Blend all together and put on top of cabbage mixture.

★It would be natural in writing a Maine cookbook, and particularly the chapter on vegetables, to save the best until last — Maine potatoes. After all those potato recipes that appeared in Cooking Down East, you would think it might not be easy to find different recipes, but it wasn't hard at all. You see, I forgot home fries or pan fries, whichever you prefer calling them, and potatoes au gratin. Then I fell heir to a different way of doing scalloped potatoes, and about that time someone sent a recipe for a jellied potato salad. This will appear in the next chapter.

There are ways of cooking potatoes in an ordinary manner that we need to think about as well. Like, if you are in a hurry and want boiled potatoes for dinner, cut them up and place in water that is already boiling. It is only going to take 10 to 15 minutes to do it in this way. Often, if in a hurry and it is baked potatoes you want, cut them in half, place on a piece of foil in your oven. This is so they do not dribble into your oven. Use a 450-degree oven and 30 minutes baking time.

PAN-FRIED POTATOES

Use a heavy frying pan. Put 3 or 4 tablespoons fat in pan to melt over a medium heat. When hot, slice cold boiled potatoes and place in fat. Sprinkle salt and pepper over slices. As they brown, you may want to cut the slices in halves or thirds — it will give you room to add more slices. Cook until browned on one side. Using large spatula, turn, and salt and pepper and continue frying until brown. Serve piping hot.

POTATOES AU GRATIN

2 tablespoons butter or
   margarine
2 tablespoons flour
1 teaspoon salt
¼ teaspoon pepper

1½ cups milk
About ¼ pound sharp
   cheese, cut up
4 cups diced cooked
   potatoes
1 cup buttered crumbs

Make cream sauce using butter, flour, salt and pepper, adding milk slowly, cooking over a low heat and stirring until thickened. Add cut up cheese and stir until it is melted, making sure sauce is smooth.

Place diced cooked potatoes in shallow baking dish. Pour the cheese sauce over them. Top with buttered crumbs. Bake at 350 degrees for 30 minutes.

POTATO SCALLOP

Pare and slice thin the number of potatoes you will need, cook in small amount salted water in covered saucepan for about 5 minutes. In buttered casserole place

1 layer drained potato
   slices
A sprinkling of diced
   raw onions
1 layer of bread crumbs
Repeat layers

Season layers with
   salt and pepper
Dot with bits of butter
Pour enough heated milk
   into pan to about cover
   ingredients
Cover top with buttered
   crumbs

Bake slowly at about 300 degrees for 1½ to 2 hours or until potatoes are tender.

Salads & Dressings

*Let onions lurk within the bowl ... and,
scarce suspected, animate the whole*

CHAPTER SEVEN

Salads and Dressings

If you hear a woman remark, "Oh, my husband is a meat-potato-gravy man," it does not mean that is all he likes to eat. It refers to substantial meals. Fish, eggs, cheese and milk are equally important to him. Yes, and salads, too.

There is no better way to learn the history of salad making in Maine than to read through your collection of old cookbooks. Way back in the late 1800's Maine women's groups learned this was a good way of earning money for their organizations.

Such a book was published in 1887 by The L. B. B. Society of North Berwick. Apparently it met with great success, for it was revised in 1889. It was called the "Nonpareil" cookbook. It sold for twenty-five cents. They listed their lobster, chicken, potato salads and salad dressings in their section on meats and fish.

In 1910, a company of ladies in East Vassalboro met in the Friend's Church and, having organized a library movement, decided to publish a cookbook. They have a section on salads and suggest "To make it one must have a spark of genius." By this time you find fruit salad, summer salad, even oyster salad, tomato and olive salad, asparagus and cucumber salad. Apparently the ladies of East Vassalboro were not making salads with plain gelatin yet, but they were well on their way to making salads a part of meal planning.

It is unusual for a day to pass now when you don't serve some kind of salad to your family. There are so many possibilities for salads that it is fertile ground for you to use your imagination. Maybe you should also keep in mind that if a salad is a thing of beauty, it is certain to have greater appeal to your family.

★There is no question but what a molded salad is easier on the cook. Probably the reason we find so many jellied salads at a public supper is that they are easier to carry somewhere. They may be prepared ahead, like the day before. Once turned out onto a platter and garnished, they do make a good impression. That is, supposing you had good success in turning your salad out of the mold.

A molded salad would always be my choice, but don't expect this to be universal. Most people choose tossed salad first, or three-bean salad. A potato salad is always popular but so is coleslaw, even if it looks kind of sloppy in the bowl.

So how come I use jellied potato salad first in this chapter on salads and dressings? Because it is made with Maine potatoes and it happens to be an excellent salad.

JELLIED MAINE
POTATO SALAD

2½ cups diced, hot, cooked   1½ teaspoons salt
   potatoes   Dash of pepper
2 teaspoons minced onion   6 tablespoons vinegar
2 tablespoons salad oil

Mix first five ingredients and 3 tablespoons of the vinegar. Let stand for a half hour to marinate, stirring once or twice. In meantime, dissolve

One 3-ounce package   1¼ cups boiling water and
   lemon gelatin   remaining 3 tablespoons
                                     vinegar

Remove about two-thirds of the gelatin mixture and add 3 tablespoons cold water. Pour just this amount of gelatin into a 9 x 5 x 3-inch loaf pan. Oil the pan first, using a piece of paper toweling for this; it means easier removal of salad when ready for unmolding.

Chill until slightly thickened. Have a hard-cooked egg ready and lay three slices of egg in pan in thickened gelatin. Save rest of egg. Add some strips of green pepper and strips of pimiento. When loaf is turned out of pan these will make a colorful topping. Return pan to refrigerator for mixture to become firm.

Chill that remaining lemon gelatin mixture; when slightly thickened, whip until fluffy. Fold into the marinated potato and add

2 tablespoons diced green pepper	¼ cup sliced radishes
1 cup finely diced celery	½ cup mayonnaise
	Remaining hard-cooked egg, chopped

Carefully spread all over decorated gelatin in loaf pan. Chill until firm, like all day or overnight. Unmold onto a platter of salad greens. Garnish with deviled eggs, raw vegetables and ripe olives. Serves 8.

★Copper pennies is an interesting name for a spiced carrot salad. This salad is prepared 24 hours ahead and if you happen to have a glass bowl, line it with lovely green lettuce leaves, turn in the copper pennies, a sprinkling of parsley on top and bring to your dinner table with great pride.

COPPER PENNIES

8-ounce jar sweet pickled onions	Mix together:
1 green pepper	1 can tomato soup
Pare, slice and cook	½ cup salad oil
2 pounds carrots	1 cup sugar
	1 teaspoon dry mustard
	Simmer for 5 minutes.

Drain juice from jar of onions. Add vinegar to the onion juice to make three-quarters cupful. Add this to tomato soup mixture, simmer a few minutes. Before removing from heat, add onions, the green pepper cut in small pieces, and the drained cooked carrots. Mix thoroughly. Store 24 hours or overnight. Serves 12.

★It is interesting that recipes can become standards in a few short years. Just like Waldorf salad, tossed salad, and potato salad, now we think also of 3-bean salad and macaroni salad. They are usually made a day ahead, too, and most housewives like that sort of preparation.

3-BEAN SALAD

One 16-ounce can cut
  green beans
One 16-ounce can
  wax beans
One 16-ounce can
  kidney beans

½ cup diced green pepper
½ cup diced or slivered
  celery
½ cup finely chopped onion

Open cans of beans and rinse them thoroughly. These kidney beans are not baked but canned boiled kidney beans. Mix all beans with the green pepper, celery and onion. Mix with the following dressing:

DRESSING FOR 3-BEAN SALAD

2/3 cup vinegar
2/3 cup sugar
1/3 cup salad oil

1 teaspoon salt
½ teaspoon black pepper

Stir dressing well, so sugar will dissolve. Turn dressing over vegetables, stir to mix well. Cover bowl, place in refrigerator for 24 hours. Serve on a bed of lettuce. Serves 8.

MACARONI SALAD

2 cups elbow macaroni
½ cup mayonnaise
1 tablespoon lemon juice
1 teaspoon salt
1 teaspoon sugar

¼ teaspoon diced pimiento
¼ teaspoon celery seed
¼ cup diced green pepper
1 cup finely diced celery
1 slice onion, finely minced

Cook elbow macaroni, rinse with cold water and drain. Mix mayonnaise with lemon juice, salt and sugar. Combine cooked macaroni, vegetables, celery seed and mayonnaise mixture, blending thoroughly. This may be stored covered in refrigerator for overnight or all day. You may want to add other seasonings, such as chopped dill pickle or chopped sweet pickle. Chopped cucumber and chopped fresh tomato add interesting flavors, too.

Serve on crisp lettuce leaves. This recipe makes 6 to 8 servings.

★Kennebec is a favorite salad. Serve it with fish or cheese and, because it has 4 hard-cooked eggs in it, you may decide it is a meal in itself, which it is.

KENNEBEC SALAD

Mash one clove garlic in a salad bowl, then discard the garlic. Add 1 teaspoon salt, 3 tablespoons vinegar, a dash of tabasco, ½ cup salad oil, 1 teaspoon dry mustard and ¼ teaspoon pepper. Combine this dressing in the bowl, using a fork for mixing. Slice one onion into bowl, making these very thin slices. Slice four hard-cooked eggs into bowl. Mix these with the dressing. Break one large head or two small heads of lettuce into bowl, making about 2-inch pieces. Toss lightly in the dressing and serve. Serves 8.

★Come summertime, Maine women try to come up with just the right idea for supper. Easy and different is the answer our Topsham friend has for us. She tells us that if the family has been blueberrying, then this is what they like to come home to. Because it has been their family favorite for years, it has an interesting name.

TEST OF TIME
SALAD BOWL

1½ cups uncooked elbow
   macaroni
6 cups boiling water
3 teaspoons salt
8 frankfurters (1 pound)
½ cup well-seasoned
   French dressing (use
   bottled, if you wish)
2 tablespoons minced
   onion
3 teaspoons lemon juice

¼ cup diced celery
½ cup coarsely diced
   cucumber
2 tablespoons slivered
   green pepper
1 cup coarsely diced
   tomatoes
½ cup mayonnaise
Speck of black pepper
About ½ head shredded
   lettuce

Cook macaroni in boiling salted water until tender. About 5 minutes before macaroni is done, add frankfurters. Cook 5 minutes longer, then drain. Remove franks and cut in bite size pieces. Combine with drained macaroni.

Add French dressing, onion and lemon juice. Chill all day or overnight or until mixture has a chance to mellow. Just before serving, toss with remaining ingredients, including the shredded lettuce. Add salt to taste. This recipe will serve 8.

SPINACH SALAD

2/3 cup French dressing
3 hard-cooked eggs
1 clove garlic

8 slices bacon, fried crisp
1 pound tender, young spinach, washed and dried

Cut garlic clove in half. Soak in the French dressing. Tear the fresh spinach into small pieces, using your fingers, discarding the stems.

Chop the egg whites, push the hard-cooked egg yolks through a sieve. Crumble the bacon. Sprinkle the eggs over the spinach in salad bowl. Mix lightly with French dressing, from which you have removed garlic.

LOW SODIUM MAYONNAISE

1 egg yolk
Few grains cayenne pepper
½ teaspoon dry mustard
½ teaspoon sugar

1¼ tablespoons vinegar
¾ tablespoon lemon juice
1 cup salad oil

Place egg yolk in deep bowl. Mix dry ingredients together. Stir into egg yolk. Stir in vinegar and lemon juice, add drop or two of oil. Beat in with fork or egg beater. Continue adding oil a few drops at a time.

Beat vigorously after each addition until about ¼ of the oil has been used. A wire whisk is wonderful for making mayonnaise. Beat in remaining oil, 1 or 2 tablespoons at a time. If it is too thick, add a little lemon juice. Store immediately in covered container in refrigerator.

POPPY SEED DRESSING

1½ cups sugar
2 teaspoons dry mustard
2 teaspoons salt
2/3 cup vinegar

2 teaspoons grated onion
2 cups salad oil
1 tablespoon poppy seeds

This delicious dressing is perfect for fruit salads. Originally intended for sliced avocado and grapefruit sections salad, you will find other salads for which it is just right.

Combine the first 5 ingredients, beat with an egg beater. Add salad oil slowly and fold in the poppy seeds. My first recipe for this called for 3 tablespoons poppy seeds. Use your own judgment. Arrange individual salads of avocado and grapefruit. Garnish with strips of pimiento. Spoon poppy seed dressing over each salad.

★Call it rhubarb sauce if you wish, but have you ever noticed that a lot of cooks refer to stewed rhubarb? Probably that is old-fashioned but it is nice, isn't it? In Maine, the double boiler method of cooking it is used. After all, it is such a simple way to make it.

STEWED RHUBARB

1 quart cut-up rhubarb   **About 1 cup sugar**
¼ teaspoon salt

Cut off leaf and root ends of rhubarb. Wash. Cut into 1-inch pieces without peeling. Measure 1 quart, turn into top of double boiler. Add salt, turn sugar over top of rhubarb. Cover and place over boiling water. Cook over low heat for 1 hour, stir when half done to mix with sugar. Remove from heat; when cool, place in refrigerator.

You might decide to cut down on the amount of sugar and when you remove the stewed rhubarb from the heat, add about one-third of a package of strawberry gelatin, dry, stirring well, so it will dissolve. Serves 6.

Stewed rhubarb is good as a breakfast fruit or as a dessert. It appears in this chapter because it is easy to place sauce dishes of rhubarb at each place for dinner and simply say, "This is your salad."

SURPRISE SALAD

2 three-ounce packages   **3 or 4 drops tabasco**
  raspberry gelatin   **sauce**
Two 16-ounce cans   **7/8 cup boiling water**
  stewed tomatoes

Place raspberry gelatin in a bowl, add boiling water. Stir to dissolve gelatin. Add canned stewed tomatoes and break up into small pieces. You find these in the markets this way — look for the word "stewed" on the can; they have other seasonings added. Turn mixture into shallow glass pan, 7 x 11. Chill until firm. Serve in squares on lettuce with a dollop of mayonnaise. Serves 10 to 12.

SLICE-YOUR-OWN-SALAD

One 16-ounce can sliced pineapple

One 3-ounce package strawberry or raspberry or lime gelatin

Remove top from can of sliced pineapple, completely. Drain. Leave slices in can. Heat pineapple juice, mix with gelatin. Stir until dissolved. Cool, pour back into can. Let set a while, then use a fork and lift slices of pineapple to allow gelatin mixture to get in between slices.

Place can in refrigerator, allow to set overnight. When ready to serve, remove other end of can. Shake salad out of can. Slice with knife between slices of pineapple. Serve on lettuce with mayonnaise.

SPRINGTIME COTTAGE CHEESE SALAD

One 3-ounce package lime gelatin
1 cup boiling water
Place gelatin in bowl, add boiling water, stir to dissolve gelatin. Place in refrigerator until thickened.

Then add:
1 cup mayonnaise
1 cup small curd cottage cheese
½ cup grated raw carrot
½ cup cucumber, cut in tiny pieces
1 teaspoon grated onion

Mix well, then return to refrigerator to chill until firm. Serve on lettuce, with a dab of mayonnaise if you wish. This salad mixture may be turned into a mold to chill until firm, or it may be chilled in a bowl and spooned onto the lettuce. Serves 6.

JELLIED GREEN SALAD

One 30-ounce can fruit
  cocktail
One 3-ounce package
  lime gelatin

One 3-ounce package
  cream cheese
1 cup cream, to whip, or
  1 pint whipped topping

Use a 7 x 11-inch glass casserole. Drain juice from fruit and spread drained fruit in glass dish. If you prefer, use a ring mold. Cut firm cream cheese into bits and dot all over top of fruit. Place in refrigerator until topping is ready to go on.

Prepare lime gelatin by heating the fruit juice with enough water to make one cup. Bring to boil, pour into lime gelatin in a bowl. Stir to dissolve gelatin. Add three-quarters cup cold water, stir to mix, then place in refrigerator until it thickens.

Whip 1 cup cream, using all-purpose or heavy cream. If you are watching calories, then use 1 pint whipped topping. Add a bit of green food coloring to this mixture after you have folded gelatin and whipped cream together. It will be a nicer shade of green.

Turn over fruit in pan; using a knife, swirl top. Place in refrigerator until firm. Cut in squares, place on lettuce with a bit of mayonnaise added. Serve this with chowder and hot yeast rolls for a delicious luncheon or supper. Serves 8.

LEMON N' LIME SALAD

One 3-ounce package
  lemon gelatin
One 3-ounce package
  lime gelatin
2 cups boiling water
One 16-ounce can crushed
  pineapple, undrained

1 cup evaporated milk
1 cup small curd
  cottage cheese
1 cup finely chopped pecans
1 tablespoon horse-radish
1 cup mayonnaise

Dissolve gelatin in boiling water. Add pineapple, stir to mix well. Place in refrigerator and chill until thickened. Fold in cottage cheese; increase to 1½ cups if you prefer to omit nuts. Add evaporated milk, horse-radish and mayonnaise. Turn into oiled mold. Chill. Turn onto a bed of endive. Serves 12. No dressing is needed — it is built into this salad.

★This easily concocted molded salad has a flavor all its own. Peach gelatin is not always available; substitute orange or lemon. Finely minced celery may be substituted for water chestnuts, too.

MANDARIN SALAD

One 3-ounce package
   peach gelatin
1 cup boiling water

One 11-ounce can
   mandarin orange sections
One 5-ounce can water
   chestnuts

Dissolve gelatin in boiling water. Drain juice from orange sections, add enough cold water to make 1 cup liquid. Stir into gelatin. Chill until it thickens but does not set. Drain the water chestnuts and chop fine. Fold these and mandarin sections into gelatin mixture. Pour into 3-cup salad mold. Chill until set. Unmold onto a bed of salad greens. Serve with a sharp French dressing or mayonnaise. Serves 6.

APPLE N' RASPBERRY SALAD

One 3-ounce package
   raspberry gelatin

1 cup applesauce
One 10-ounce package
   frozen raspberries

Thaw raspberries so they will be partially thawed when added to ingredients. Heat applesauce, add dry gelatin to this, stirring until dissolved. Add partially thawed raspberries and stir until they are thawed. The mixture will thicken as you stir. Turn into mold and chill. Serves 6. This may also be used for a dessert, if you would rather. If using for a salad, mold in 6 custard cups, rinsing them with cold water before turning salad mixture into them. Serve on lettuce with mayonnaise. This makes a tart salad.

★This salad dressing came from Down East and you will like it for jellied salads, especially of the fruit variety. It is not a cooked dressing and is easily prepared.

SALAD DRESSING

1 teaspoon salt	2 egg yolks, beaten
2 teaspoons dry mustard	1 can condensed milk
1 cup vinegar (scant	(sweetened)
the measure)	2 egg whites, beaten stiff
1 stick margarine, melted	

Mix the dry ingredients, add milk, beaten egg yolks, then melted margarine, beating mixture together. Very slowly, add vinegar. This becomes thick. Lastly, fold in the beaten egg whites. Turn into covered jar and keep refrigerated.

RED, WHITE AND GREEN SALAD

RED LAYER

One 3-ounce package   One 1-pound can whole
   strawberry gelatin   cranberry sauce

Dissolve gelatin in one and one-eighth cups boiling water. Add can whole cranberry sauce, stir to mix well. Chill until partly set. Turn into large ring mold or two loaf tins. Allow to set.

WHITE LAYER

One 3-ounce package   1 cup crushed pineapple
   lemon gelatin   plus juice
One 8-ounce package   ¼ cup finely chopped
   cream cheese   pecans

Dissolve gelatin in 1¼ cups boiling water. Add cream cheese and beat with egg beater until smooth. Add pineapple with syrup and finely chopped pecans. Chill until partly set, then turn over red layer.

GREEN LAYER

One 3-ounce package   2 cups canned grapefruit
   lime gelatin   sections, cut fine
2 tablespoons sugar   (a 16-ounce can)

Dissolve lime gelatin in 1 cup boiling water. Add sugar and grapefruit bits; it will not make any difference if some of this syrup gets into mixture, too. Chill this mixture until partly set, then turn over white layer. Allow salad to set overnight.

This salad will serve 12 to 16 people. I like it best when done in 2 loaf pans. It cuts so easily.

★Cranberry apples have everything going for them. First, you will use Maine Macs. You may even live in a part of Maine where you pick your own cranberries. But they may be prepared two or three days ahead of when you intend serving them — just keep them refrigerated. They are so impressive and taste so good that you will make them often.

CRANBERRY APPLES

1 cup sugar	Red food coloring
3 cups water	8 medium sized MacIntosh
2 cups cranberries	apples, cored and pared

Cook 1 cup sugar and 1 cup of the water for 5 minutes, using a good-sized saucepan. Add the cranberries, cover and simmer over a medium heat until the cranberries pop. Remove about one-half of the cranberries, plus some of the juice, for this will be used to fill the cooked apples.

To the remaining sauce add the 2 cups water, plus some red food coloring — not too much — and simmer about 5 minutes. Strain, then add the apples. Leaving cover off, cook the apples on medium heat, baste and turn once or twice, and test with fork for doneness.

As each apple is done, place on a platter and fill center with reserved cranberries and syrup. Chill and serve either as a salad or around a platter of cold meat.

All Kinds of Breads

*The very staff of life; the comfort of
the husband, the pride of the wife*

CHAPTER EIGHT

All Kinds of Breads

Bread making heads the list when we listen to the talk about the return to basics in the kitchen. It would be hard to convince Maine cooks, however, that we had ever given it up, for we have kept on making all kinds of bread.

You realize this when the old expression like "being in the dough dish" or "I was up to my elbows in flour" have persisted all through the years.

Probably no other baking brings such personal satisfaction as taking a pan of biscuits from the oven. Or removing hot muffins from tins, to place before the admiring eyes of the family. Then when loaves of freshly baked bread are turned from pans, it becomes a whole new world for cook and family alike.

With so much leisure time there has been a stampede to the kitchen, and family life is right back where it used to be. The kitchen of today is where family members want to be, anyway, for this is where the action is ; large or small, the kitchen has become the center of the house.

And guess who wants to get his hands in the dough dish? The man of the house. And thinking back, I cannot recall any of the men down at New Meadows as I was growing up who ever made bread. They were too busy farming. But believe me, I can name dozens of men nowadays who make bread.

It all has to do with that leisure time, and what better place to be in than the kitchen. Certainly no one is going to find fault with anyone who turns out a loaf of freshly baked bread.

★Every so often a recipe comes along that seems just right. One-Loaf White Yeast Bread is that kind of a recipe.

For the cook who wants to make only one loaf of bread or cannot do any kneading or is making yeast bread for the very first time, this recipe will be the one.

ONE-LOAF
WHITE YEAST BREAD

1 ¼ cups warm water
1 envelope dry yeast
2 tablespoons soft
    shortening or oil

2 teaspoons salt
2 tablespoons sugar
3 cups flour, unsifted

In mixing bowl, dissolve yeast in warm water. Add shortening or oil, salt and sugar. Measuring flour into cup by spoonfuls to avoid packing down flour, stir in one-half of amount called for; keep in mind that brands of flour vary and you might need more or less than the 3 cups.

Stir the batter until smooth, then add remaining flour, stir and scrape down sides of bowl. When yeast dough has taken all the flour it can, cover bowl with cloth. Let dough rise until double in size; this will take about one hour.

Beat dough about 25 strokes, then spread evenly in greased loaf pan, 9 x 5 x 3 inches. Cover pan with cloth and allow to rise in pan until dough is about ½-inch from top. It will be slightly higher in center. This takes about 1 hour longer.

Bake at 450 degrees for 10 minutes, lower heat to 325 degrees and bake 25 minutes longer. Turn loaf of yeast bread onto rack, butter top of loaf, cool and store.

It is as easy as that. Because I am in the habit of doing so, when the yeast dough has risen in the bowl, I turn it out onto a lightly floured board, whack down the dough using the edge of my hand, allow it to rest for 10 minutes, then knead it a few times, shape it into a loaf, then place it in the greased pan. It is not necessary to do this, however.

★This recipe for oatmeal bread has a bit of a twist. A cup of hot coffee is added to this yeast bread. It adds a bit of color and good flavor. A recipe from the coast of Maine — Rockland.

OATMEAL BREAD

¾ cup boiling water
1 cup hot coffee
1 cup rolled oats or
 oatmeal
1/3 cup shortening
½ cup molasses

3 teaspoons salt
2 envelopes dry yeast
¼ cup lukewarm water
2 eggs, slightly beaten
5½ cups sifted flour

Combine boiling water, hot coffee (which may be made with instant coffee), rolled oats, shortening, molasses and salt. Cool to lukewarm.

Add yeast to lukewarm water, stir to dissolve and when first mixture is cooled to lukewarm, add yeast. Add slightly beaten eggs. Add flour gradually, stirring until dough will take no more of flour. Place in greased bowl. Cover. Place in refrigerator for 2 hours.

Shape chilled dough into 2 loaves. You could knead this dough if you wish before placing these loaves in pans, but it is not necessary. Let rise in a warm place, as you do all yeast products. This takes about 2 hours or until the loaves are doubled in size. Bake 1 hour at 350 degrees. Turn onto rack to cool; while still hot brush tops with butter.

★This standard recipe for making two loaves of white yeast bread is the one I always used until several years ago when the recipe for yeast bread in Cooking Down East was given to me. That is the one I use now. It makes three loaves and the recipe calls for oil. Yet every once in a while, because I feel nostalgic, I make this old standard yeast bread.

HOMEMADE BREAD

1 cup milk
1 cup hot water
2 teaspoons salt
2 tablespoons sugar
2 tablespoons shortening

1 yeast cake or 1 envelope
 dry yeast
¼ cup lukewarm water
About 6 cups sifted
 flour

Scald milk. Put salt, sugar, shortening and hot water into mixing bowl, add scalded milk and stir until shortening is melted. Cool until lukewarm. Mix yeast and lukewarm water and stir, so it will dissolve. Combine the mixtures, then add flour by cupfuls, mixing after each addition until dough can be turned out onto a floured board to knead. Knead until dough feels smooth and satiny, which takes about 8 to 10 minutes. You will develop your own kneading technique; how you do it does not matter — just knead. Shape dough into a smooth ball. Place in a greased bowl, cover with a damp towel, and let rise in a warm place until double in bulk.

Punch dough down and let rise again until doubled. Knead dough down, turn onto floured board and divide in two equal portions. Round up each portion into a smooth ball, cover with towel, and let rise on board about 15 minutes. This gives the dough a chance to rest. Shape each ball into a loaf and place in greased bread pan. If you have them, then I am sure you feel your teflon bread pans are your prize baking utensil. No greasing and needing only to be wiped out after using, they are a joy to own.

Again, cover pans of dough and allow to double in size. Bake at 450 degrees for 10 minutes; reduce heat and allow to bake at 325 degrees for 25 minutes. Or, bake at 400 degrees for 45 minutes.

Turn bread onto racks to cool. Butter the tops, store in plastic bags. Bread freezes very well. When removed from freezer, let it thaw in bag. This makes it more moist and it tastes exactly like freshly baked bread.

WONDERFUL CHEESE BREAD

1 cup hot water
¼ cup sugar
1½ teaspoons salt
1 yeast cake or 1 envelope
   dry yeast
2 tablespoons lukewarm
   water

1 teaspoon sugar
1 egg, well beaten
2 cups grated American
   cheese
3 to 4 cups sifted flour

Combine the hot water with the ¼ cup sugar and the salt. Cool until lukewarm. Meanwhile, soften yeast in the 2 tablespoons lukewarm water; add the teaspoon sugar, stir to mix well, then add to the first mixture. Add beaten egg, grated cheese and as much of the flour as can be stirred into the dough without kneading. Then turn onto a floured board, knead until it can be easily handled. Shape into one loaf, place in well-greased loaf pan, about 9 x 5 x 3. Cover and allow to rise in a warm place until double in bulk. Bake at 375 degrees about 45 minutes. Remove from pan, butter top of loaf. Cool on rack and store.

If you have never eaten a sliced cold meat sandwich made with cheese bread, nor eaten a slice of cheese bread toasted, what a treat you have in store for you. Especially when the taste treat is of your own making. Grate the cheese yourself if you wish, but it will be easier if you buy grated American cheese.

★One loaf white yeast bread is the answer to cooks who are trying their hand at bread making, but how about yeast rolls? The answer to this one is to make 90-Minute Rolls. It holds true, too. Time them, yourself. This recipe makes one dozen, and that is good many times if your family is small.

90-MINUTE YEAST ROLLS

1 yeast cake or 1 envelope dry yeast, dissolved in 1/3 cup lukewarm water	½ teaspoon salt 2 tablespoons melted shortening
½ cup lukewarm milk	1 tablespoon sugar 2 cups flour, unsifted

Dissolve yeast in lukewarm water. Heat milk to lukewarm, add salt, melted shortening or oil, sugar and yeast that has been dissolved in 1/3 cup lukewarm water. Stir to mix well. Measure flour into cup by spoonfuls, since it is unsifted and you do not want to pack it down in measuring cup. Add the 2 cupfuls, stirring to mix well. Cover, let rise 50 minutes. Stir down, turn onto lightly floured board or use wax paper, knead lightly.

At this point the shape of the yeast rolls depends upon you. It could be that you will decide to divide the dough into 12 portions, shaping them into balls that will fit into each section of muffin pans. You could make each of the 12 portions into 3 tiny balls for each section of your muffin tin and you would have clover-leaf rolls.

The chef at the Parker House in Boston who long ago folded his yeast roll dough he had rolled out and cut with a biscuit cutter to make a pocketbook type of roll made himself famous as well as his hotel. To this day a folded type roll is always known as a Parker House roll.

This is what we will do with our 90-Minute roll dough. Having kneaded it quickly, roll with rolling pin. Use a biscuit cutter to cut 12 rounds. Have melted margarine ready; dip one-half of the round into it, fold over, place in greased pan. A bread pan works well for it will hold just the 12 rolls and, once baked, each roll is crusty.

Cover pan, let rise for 20 minutes. Bake at 400 degrees for 20 minutes. Makes 1 dozen.

★These are the days when Hot Cross Buns appear in our markets the very day the Lenten season begins, if not before. Remembering how one of the large display windows at the old Frost and Smith's Bakery Shop in Brunswick looked the morning of Good Friday long ago, I cannot help but share this nostalgic moment with you.

We just did not see Hot Cross Buns until that morning. All day long the freshly baked buns were placed in the window and all day long a steady file of customers came into the bake shop to buy their supply for supper from the display in the window — row upon row of Hot Cross Buns. Before the days of packaging, you gave your order and your rolls were placed in white paper bags, in half dozen, dozen or two dozen lots. Sometimes you ordered two to be placed in a small paper bag and you ate them as you walked up Maine Street.

Now you can make your own Hot Cross Buns for your family to enjoy at any time during the Lenten season. Another recipe from our friend who has shared so many with us.

HOT CROSS BUNS

1 cup milk	1 egg, well beaten
¼ cup sugar	¼ teaspoon cinnamon
2 tablespoons butter	½ cup seedless raisins
½ teaspoon salt	¼ cup currants
1 yeast cake or 1 envelope dry yeast	If you wish, ½ cup finely shredded citron
¼ cup lukewarm water	3 cups flour (unsifted)

Scald milk. Stir yeast into lukewarm water. Combine scalded milk with sugar, butter and salt; stir until dissolved and butter is melted. Add dissolved yeast. Add well-beaten egg, cinnamon, raisins and currants. Measure flour into measuring cup by spoonfuls so it will not be packed down. Add as much flour as can be stirred into dough; brands of flour vary so you may need a little more or less. Cover bowl, let rise in a warm place until doubled.

Turn onto a lightly floured board, knead a few times, break off dough and form into buns. Have some melted butter ready and coat each bun lightly. Place buns in a greased pan or pans. Cover. Allow to rise until doubled in bulk. Bake at 375 degrees for 15 to 20 minutes. This makes 2 dozen buns.

After placing buns in pan for rising, take kitchen scissors and gently snip a cross in top of each bun. This will make it easier to ice the cross after the buns have been baked and cooled slightly.

To make icing: Use about ¾ cup confectioners' sugar, mixed with a little milk. Use a teaspoon to dribble the cross on top of each bun. These are best when served fragrant and warm.

★A quart of buttermilk in your refrigerator will provide you with an ingredient to use in present day recipes that give an old-fashioned flavor. Actually, a quart of buttermilk on hand can make you "drunk with power" as there are so many ways in which it may be used. If you do have buttermilk, then you can feel quite heavenly, for you will be able to make Angel Biscuits.

This recipe is made with yeast as well as buttermilk, so you have a great flavor combined with lightness and a simple procedure for making this hot bread, for there is no rising of the dough. Best of all, it makes 3 dozen.

ANGEL BISCUITS

1 yeast cake or 1 envelope dry yeast	2 teaspoons baking powder
	1 teaspoon soda
2 tablespoons lukewarm water	1 teaspoon salt
	1 cup shortening
5 cups flour, unsifted	2 cups buttermilk
¼ cup sugar	

Dissolve yeast in lukewarm water and let stand 5 minutes.

Measure flour into cup by spoonfuls. Sift flour, sugar, baking powder, soda and salt. Using pastry blender or 2 knives, cut shortening into sifted dry ingredients. Add buttermilk and dissolved yeast and mix well. Turn onto floured board, knead 2 or 3 times, roll to desired thickness. Cut into biscuits, dip into melted margarine. Fold over like Parker House rolls or place flat biscuits in greased pan.

Bake at 450 degrees for 12 minutes. This recipe makes 3 dozen regular size biscuits. If you do not want to bake all at once, place in 2 pans, one for baking now. Slide the other unbaked into a plastic bag, seal, place in freezer for baking at a later time. When you do this, bring to room temperature, which will allow the biscuits to thaw, then bake as in directions.

★It is not hard to recall the very first time I ever ate these biscuits — it was a hot summer's night and they were served with a salad. It has been many years since this family lived in Augusta but I like to think of the fine gift our hostess left us by sharing her unusual biscuit recipe. I say this because it has three leavening agents—soda, cream of tartar and baking powder. I make these biscuits when I have buttermilk on hand.

This reminds me. If you have an old-fashioned recipe calling for sour milk, you realize, of course, that you may substitute an equal amount of buttermilk. If you are with-out either, then add 1 tablespoon of vinegar or lemon juice to 1 cup of sweet milk.

BUTTERMILK BISCUITS

2 cups sifted flour
¼ teaspoon salt
1 teaspoon soda
2 teaspoons cream
  of tartar
1½ teaspoons baking
  powder

2 rounding tablespoons
  shortening
1 cup buttermilk

Sift flour, measure and sift together with salt, soda, cream of tartar and baking powder. Cut in the shortening, using a pastry blender or 2 knives. Add the buttermilk quickly, using a fork for stirring into dry ingredients. Knead lightly on a floured board.

Cut in size biscuits desired, place on a greased pan, and bake at 475 degrees for 10 to 12 minutes.

★Sometimes you wonder how you can miss out on using a product that has been on the market for years. Now, there is nothing new about Bakewell Cream, which is a substitute for cream of tartar. In Maine, we use cream of tartar and soda for leavening agents in many of our recipes, particularly the old ones. It is a sort of heritage we pass along to others. You will find this combination in many of the recipes in this cookbook.

Finally I listened to enough Maine cooks tell me about how good it is to use Bakewell Cream in all recipes calling for cream of tartar. You see, they have been using it for years; well, at least some of them have. Now, most of us have a can of Bakewell Cream in our cupboards.

OLD-FASHIONED
BAKEWELL CREAM BISCUITS

4 cups sifted flour
4 teaspoons Bakewell
  Cream
2 teaspoons soda

1 teaspoon salt
½ cup shortening
1½ cups milk

This amount makes 24 biscuits, but you may halve it easily.

Mix and sift first 4 ingredients. Add shortening and cut in, using pastry blender or 2 knives. Use a vegetable shortening for these biscuits. Add milk all at once, stir quickly with a fork to make a soft dough. Turn onto a floured board, knead 5 or 6 times. Roll out ½-inch or more thick. Cut with biscuit cutter, place on ungreased cookie sheet. Top each biscuit with a little butter or milk. Bake at 475 degrees 5 minutes, turn off heat and continue to bake on stored heat until golden brown. If you prefer, bake at 450 degrees for 12 to 15 minutes. These biscuits are extra high and light.

★After my first book, "Cooking Down East," was published a young Maine cook exclaimed, "How could you forget butterfly shortcake!" Here it is this time, plus the recipe for old-fashioned shortcake which I am more apt to use.

BUTTERFLY SHORTCAKE

2 cups sifted flour	½ cup cream
4 teaspoons baking	¼ cup water
powder	½ cup shortening
¾ teaspoon salt	
1/3 cup sugar	

This is a short, soft dough which will be dropped onto the baking sheet, not rolled.

Sift flour. Measure and sift together with baking powder, sugar and salt. Add vegetable shortening by cutting into dry ingredients, using a pastry blender. Mix ½ cup cream with ¼ cup cold water, add quickly to dry ingredients, stirring with a fork.

Drop by large spoonfuls onto ungreased pan or cookie sheeet 2 inches apart. Bake at 450 degrees for about 15 minutes. Why the name butterfly? Have the sweetened strawberries ready. If you use cream — which is not necessary — have that whipped. Use soup plates preferably. Take each shortcake, break in two so you have 2 complete halves, arrange shortcake like butterfly wings, arrange strawberries in and around broken-in-two shortcake. Top with whipped cream or plain cream. Or none.

OLD FASHIONED STRAWBERRY SHORTCAKE

2 cups sifted flour
1 teaspoon soda
2 teaspoons cream of
  tartar
½ teaspoon salt

1 stick butter or
  margarine
1 egg
About 2/3 cup milk

Sift flour, measure and sift together with soda, cream of tartar and salt. You could use 4 teaspoons baking powder if you do not have soda and cream of tartar. Blend in butter or margarine, using pastry blender. Beat egg slightly, combine with milk, add all at once to dry ingredients. Stir with a fork. Toss dough onto lightly floured board. Divide in halves. Roll or pat very gently and place one half in a buttered 8-inch circular baking pan. Brush that half with melted butter. Place other half on top. Bake at 450 degrees until shortcake is delicately browned, about 12 to 15 minutes.

Crush 1 quart washed, hulled and drained strawberries, add 1 cup sugar. Whip 1 cup cream. When shortcake is baked, split it, place bottom half cut side up on a platter or large plate. Cover with crushed strawberries. Lay second round cut side up on top. Cover with remainder of strawberries. Spoon on the cream. Top with whole strawberries. Serve at once, cut in pie-shaped wedges. This is a case of "do as I say, not as I do," because this is what you will do if you want a real old-fashioned strawberry shortcake. I use this recipe, for it is a real biscuit shortcake. Instead of making 2 big layers, I cut the rolled-out dough with my largest 3-inch cookie cutter, bake the shortcakes on a cookie sheet, and serve them in soup plates.

TWIN MOUNTAIN MUFFINS

2 cups sifted flour
3 teaspoons baking
  powder
½ teaspoon salt
2 tablespoons sugar

1 cup milk
2 tablespoons melted
  butter or vegetable oil
1 egg, well beaten

Sift flour, measure and sift together with baking powder, salt and sugar. Combine egg, milk and melted butter or oil. Turn into dry ingredients, mixing only enough to dampen flour. Spoon into greased muffin pans. Makes 12 muffins. Bake at 400 degrees for 25 minutes.

Actually these are plain muffins, and if you want to make true twin-mountain muffins, you double the amount of sugar and butter or oil.

CRANBERRY MUFFINS

1 cup chopped raw cranberries	¼ cup sugar
½ cup sugar	1 egg, slightly beaten
2 cups sifted flour	¾ cup sour milk or buttermilk
¼ teaspoon salt	4 tablespoons melted shortening
¾ teaspoon soda	

Using a chopping bowl and chopping knife, chop the raw cranberries. Measure 1 cup, combine with the ½ cup sugar, set aside.

Measure sifted flour and sift together with salt, soda and the ¼ cup sugar. Sift into mixing bowl. Beat 1 egg slightly, combine with sour milk or buttermilk and melted shortening. Add to dry ingredients, mix lightly until flour disappears. Gently fold in the chopped cranberry mixture. Fill greased muffin tins two-thirds full. Makes 12 muffins. Bake at 400 degrees for 20 minutes.

BRAN MUFFINS

1 cup whole bran cereal	½ teaspoon salt
1 cup sifted flour	1 egg
¼ cup sugar	1 cup milk
3 teaspoons baking powder	¼ cup vegetable oil

Sift flour, sugar, baking powder and salt into a bowl. Stir in the bran cereal. In a medium bowl and using a fork, beat the egg slightly, add milk and oil. Add egg mixture all at once to flour mixture. Using a spoon, stir until flour is moistened. The batter will be lumpy. Spoon into greased muffin tins. Makes 12 muffins. Bake at 400 degrees for 25 minutes until golden brown.

★Cheese and bacon muffins disappear "like mist before the sun" when they appear in the Coffee Shop at the Augusta General Hospital on Wednesday mornings. It is a privilege to have this recipe to share with you from the Coffee Shop Volunteer who originated this recipe. It would not be unusual, for she is that kind of a cook.

CHEESE AND BACON MUFFINS

Fry 1/4 to 1/3 pound
  bacon, depending upon
  its leanness
Reserve 1/3 cup of the
  drippings
1 egg
1 cup milk

1 cup sharp cheese,
  shredded
2 cups flour, sifted
1 teaspoon salt
¼ cup sugar
3 teaspoons baking
  powder

Beat egg slightly, stir in milk, the 1/3 cup bacon fat and 1 cup shredded cheese. Set aside.

Sift together the flour, salt, sugar and baking powder. Stir into the egg mixture. Crumble the fried bacon and add to mixture. Spoon into greased muffin tins. Bake at 400 degrees for 18 to 20 minutes. Makes 12 muffins.

These muffins will provide a built-in breakfast and will be popular in your family.

MAPLE MUFFINS

2 cups flour, sifted
4 teaspoons baking
  powder
½ teaspoon salt

1 egg
½ cup milk
½ cup maple syrup
¼ cup vegetable oil

Sift dry ingredients together into a bowl. Combine egg, slightly beaten with milk, maple syrup and oil. Add liquid to dry ingredients. Mix gently. Spoon into greased muffin tins. Makes 12 muffins. Bake at 400 degrees for 18 to 20 minutes.

★You may decide to keep your maple syrup to use on griddle cakes. It surprised me a little when, after my first cookbook, someone remarked, "You forgot griddle cakes." We will not do that this time.

GRIDDLE CAKES

1 ¼ cups sifted flour
2 ½ teaspoons baking
    powder
3 tablespoons sugar
½ teaspoon salt

1 egg, beaten
¾ cup milk
3 tablespoons melted fat
    or vegetable oil

Sift flour, measure and sift with baking powder, sugar and salt. Beat egg, combine with milk and melted fat or oil. Add to dry ingredients all at once, mix until smooth.

Drop batter from a tablespoon onto a hot griddle which has been greased or not, according to manufacturers' directions. Spread the cakes out lightly using the back of the spoon. Cook on one side until puffed, full of bubbles and cooked on the edges. Turn and cook on the other side. Serve immediately.

No griddle? Don't forget about your electric sandwich toaster. Opened up, it can make a fine griddle. Four cakes can be cooked at once.

If you have maple syrup, pancakes become a special kind of treat. Remember, once the syrup is opened, keep it in the refrigerator. If you have a large amount, have been careless about its storage and find mold has developed on top, remove mold, heat syrup to boiling point and store in airtight jars or bottles.

★Popovers are show-offs. The fact that popovers are very accommodating is a help to the cook. Like putting them into a cold oven, then turning it on to bake the required number of minutes. Or having the oven heated to the proper temperature when you put the popovers in to bake. Just as fascinating will be to learn you may mix them after supper, turn the batter into well-greased custard cups, and place those on a pan in a cold oven. If you have a timer on your oven, set it to turn the oven on in the morning so the popovers will bake at that time to be ready for breakfast.

The popover recipe in "Cooking Down East" is the standard recipe and I like that, but along came one for no-beat popovers and that is good, too, as well as oatmeal popovers, which came to me one summer from a friend on Eustis Ridge.

NO BEAT POPOVERS

2 eggs   1 cup sifted flour
1 cup milk   ½ teaspoon salt

Use a muffin tin for this recipe, the 12 muffin size. Sift flour and salt together. Use your favorite mixing spoon—and I like to think it is a wooden one. Break eggs into mixing bowl. Pour in the milk, add flour and salt. Beat with spoon, just enough to mix. There will still be a big lump of flour in the batter. A quart glass measure is very good for mixing popovers, for then you may pour the batter into the muffin pan. There's no butter in the recipe, so make sure the muffin pan is liberally buttered. Fill tin to about one-half full in each section. Place pan in cold oven. If you cook electrically, turn temperature to 425 and switch to bake for about 25 minutes.

A preheated oven works well, too. Same temperature but check popovers at end of 20 minutes. Serve piping hot with butter. Did you know popovers freeze well? Try it if you ever have extras.

OATMEAL POPOVERS

1 cup sifted flour   3 eggs
¼ teaspoon salt   1½ cups milk
½ cup uncooked oatmeal

Sift together flour and salt, stir in oatmeal. Beat eggs slightly, add milk, combine with dry ingredients. Beat lightly. Turn into well-buttered custard cups. Place cups on cookie sheet. Place in cold oven, turn to 400 degrees and bake about 40 minutes. If your oven is preheated, bake at same temperature for about 35 minutes. Makes 8 good sized popovers. Serve hot.

★Quick breads baked in a loaf or, as they are sometimes referred to, tea loaves, come in all kinds and sizes. Size is referred to because sometimes these quick loaves are baked in very small loaf pans or even in tin cans for an unusual shape.

When Maine cooks talk about brown bread, our thoughts turn to steaming of this old time recipe. Had you ever thought of baking a brown bread? If you do, it becomes known as a quick bread. You could make this very quickly and easily as a last minute bread to serve with baked beans on a Saturday night.

BAKED BROWN BREAD

1 egg, lightly beaten	½ teaspoon salt
4 tablespoons sugar	1 teaspoon soda
1 cup molasses	1 cup whole wheat flour
2/3 cup buttermilk	2/3 cup seedless raisins
1 cup sifted flour	

Combine the beaten egg and sugar, blend in the molasses and stir in the buttermilk. Sift the flour with salt and soda, add whole wheat flour and raisins. Combine the wet and dry ingredients, lightly. Turn into greased 9 x 5 x 3 inch pan. Bake at 350 degrees for 1 hour. Test for doneness, using a toothpick or cake tester. Turn loaf onto rack, then place on a board, slice and serve hot.

CHEDDAR BRAN LOAF

3 tablespoons margarine	½ teaspoon salt
1/3 cup sugar	1 cup buttermilk
1 egg	1 cup cheddar cheese,
1½ cups sifted flour	shredded
1½ teaspoon baking	1 cup all-bran cereal,
powder	crushed fine
¼ teaspoon soda	

Cream margarine and sugar, add egg and beat until light and creamy. Sift flour, measure and sift together with baking powder, soda and salt. Add to creamed mixture alternately with buttermilk. Fold in the cheese and bran. Turn into well greased loaf pan, 9 x 5 x 3. Bake at 350 degrees for 1 hour. Remove from pan and cool on a rack. Store. This loaf makes delicious sandwiches and an equally wonderful slice of toast.

MAINE BLUEBERRY NUT BREAD

2 eggs
1 cup sugar
1 cup milk
3 tablespoons melted
   shortening
3 cups sifted flour

4 teaspoons baking
   powder
1 teaspoon salt
1 cup Maine blueberries
1/2 cup broken nutmeats

Beat eggs. Add sugar and beat thoroughly. Add milk and melted shortening. Sift flour, measure and sift together with baking powder and salt. Add to liquid ingredients. Stir only until blended. Fold in blueberries and nutmeats. Turn into well greased loaf pan, 9 x 5 x 3. Bake 1 hour at 350 degrees. Turn onto rack to cool. Wrap and store.

This loaf, like all loaves of quick bread, freezes very well. If you have Maine blueberries in your freezer, use these in making this loaf. When adding blueberries from the freezer, add them just as they are — frozen hard.

BLUEBERRY CORN BREAD

1 stick margarine
1 cup sugar
2 eggs
1 cup cornmeal
1 1/2 cups sifted flour

2 teaspoons baking
   powder
1/2 teaspoon salt
1 1/2 cups milk
1 cup blueberries

Cream margarine and sugar until light and fluffy. Add eggs one at a time and beat well. Add cornmeal. Sift and measure flour. Take out 2 tablespoons of the flour and dredge this on the blueberries, which are folded in last.

Sift remainder of flour with baking powder and salt. Add about one-third of the flour mixture to creamed mixture, then half of the milk, more dry ingredients, the remainder of milk, then the rest of flour mixture. Fold in the floured blueberries. Turn into greased 8 x 8-inch pan. Bake at 375 degrees for 40 minutes or until done. Cut in squares and serve hot. Serves 8.

CHERRY BREAD

2 tablespoons margarine	One 8-ounce bottle
1 cup sugar	maraschino cherries
1 egg	Milk added to juice
½ teaspoon salt	drained from cherries
2 cups sifted flour	to make
2 teaspoons baking	1 cup liquid in all
powder	

Cream margarine and sugar. Add salt. Add unbeaten egg, mix until light and fluffy.

Sift flour, measure and sift together with baking powder. Drain juice from bottle of maraschino cherries into a measuring cup. Add enough milk to this to make 1 cup liquid in all.

Add sifted dry ingredients and milk alternately to creamed mixture. Chop the drained cherries, fold into batter. No chopped nuts are called for in this recipe, but add some if you wish. Turn into well-greased loaf pan. Bake at 350 degrees for 1 hour or until it tests done. Turn loaf onto rack to cool, wrap and store. Freezes well.

★A muffin recipe that has swept the state, so to speak, is a delicious muffin. But best of all, the large amount of batter is mixed, then stored in the refrigerator, tightly covered, for up to six weeks time. An Augusta friend brought the recipe to me a few years ago when she returned from Florida.

BEST-OF-MINE MUFFINS

2 cups All-Bran	1 quart buttermilk
2 cups boiling water	4 cups Bran-Buds
1 cup, plus 3 tablespoons	6 cups flour, sifted
vegetable shortening	5 teaspoons soda
2½ cups sugar	2 teaspoons salt
4 eggs	

Pour boiling water over All-Bran and allow to set while mixing ingredients. Cream shortening and sugar. Add eggs one at a time, beating well after each addition. Blend in the quart of buttermilk. Add All-Bran and water mixture. Add the 4 cups of Bran-Buds.

Sift flour together with soda and salt. Add to mixture. Turn into large container and cover tightly. Keep refrigerated for up to 6 weeks. Do not stir, merely spoon into muffin tins as you get ready to bake muffins. Bake at 400 degrees for 16 to 20 minutes or until top is firm.

★In our town there is a woman who fries doughnuts to sell. Maybe there is in your town, also. I hope so, for it is a privilege to be able to buy homemade doughnuts. Our friend did not intend being in the doughnut business. It became a happening because someone asked if she would fry some of her delicious doughnuts for a party. That did it. From then on she was in business. But this is because she wants to do it. She was just as willing to share her recipes for this cookbook, too, and it gives you the snug feeling that in Maine, cooks just simply like to share their recipes, for others to enjoy.

WINNIE'S DOUGHNUTS

Beat:
  2 eggs
  1 cup sugar
  3 tablespoons melted
    shortening
Add:
  1 cup buttermilk

Stir in:
  3½ cups sifted flour,
    sifted together with
  ½ teaspoon nutmeg
  1 teaspoon salt
  1 teaspoon soda
  1 teaspoon baking
    powder

Store in covered container overnight in refrigerator. This dough may be kept as long as a week. Roll out dough on a floured board to ½-inch thickness and cut with floured doughnut cutter. Fry until golden brown in deep fat heated to 370 degrees. Turn doughnuts once. Makes 2½ dozen doughnuts. Drain on brown paper.

VARIATIONS

Chocolate: Add 2 envelopes liquid unsweetened chocolate and 1 teaspoon vanilla to egg mixture. Decrease flour to 3¼ cups.

Orange: Add grated rind of 1 orange. For liquid, use juice of orange and add buttermilk to make 1 cup liquid in all.

MOLASSES DOUGHNUTS

Beat:
  ½ cup molasses
  ½ cup sugar
  1 egg
  2 tablespoons melted
    shortening
Dissolve:
  1½ teaspoons soda in
  1 cup buttermilk

Add buttermilk mixture to
  egg mixture, then
  stir in:
3½ cups sifted flour,
  sifted together with
  ½ teaspoon cinnamon
  ½ teaspoon ginger
  ½ teaspoon salt

Refrigerate dough in covered container overnight, as in directions for plain doughnuts. Proceed with frying just as the directions are given in that recipe, too. Of all her choices, these have to be my favorite. Winnie tells me, though, that there is never anything halfway about molasses doughnuts; you either do or you don't like them.

Desserts

*A guest never
forgets the host
who has treated
him kindly*

CHAPTER NINE

Desserts

For generations we have been doing some enchanted eating in Maine. It is all because that is the way Maine cooks have wanted it. Tempting recipes handed down from mother to daughter didn't just happen. It was planned that way. Maine cooks are schemers — you watch them. Before you know it your piece of pie will have been cut larger than you planned. You could be eating a third or fourth cookie when one was what you had in mind.

Packaged mixes, convenience foods and the cooking short cuts available in our markets are appealing, but cooks know they can become costly. Also there is the matter of pride. Maine cooks like to keep alive the tradition of "cooking from scratch" and they hand down family recipes to provide enchanted eating.

This chapter on desserts includes many of these recipes, as well as those on the Now side. They include cakes, cookies and bars, confections, pies and puddings. You will find old favorites among them and new ones, too. You see, there is so much to talk about when we mention desserts.

You will find a scattering of holiday recipes all through this chapter. Although families establish their own customs, there are sure to be ideas from someone else you will want to adopt for your own.

Naturally, our food habits change. Some of these recipes prove this. There are remarkable food products in our markets that surpass anything we might have known. Is it any wonder that we do enchanted eating in Maine? And tomorrow there'll be more.

CAKES

★It wouldn't seem right if I didn't tell you one of my favorite verses that I have repeated so often when giving cooking schools, talks and demonstrations.

"About the bride and the cake that she baked
And of how she measured out the flour with a very
solemn air,
The salt and sugar also, and she took the greatest care
To count the eggs correctly.
And to add a little bit of baking powder,
That beginners oft omit.
Then she mixed it all together and she baked it for an hour.
But she never quite forgave herself, for leaving
out the flour."
Anonymous.

Your cake baking success will be due in great part to the kind of pans you use. Shiny pans give best results. You will want to keep away from old darkened pans, from enamel, and from glass in cake baking. If you do use a glass pan, lower the recommended temperature by 25 degrees.

These pans just mentioned absorb heat faster than shiny pans, and the sides and bottom of cakes get too hard and brown as they bake. But if you are baking a pie, a glass pan gives best results.

★Probably this cake recipe has been in my files as long as any, and I am certain I have made more of them than any other cake of this type. A combination of sponge cake and angel cake in marbled effect will conjure up thoughts of the past, and you will find it a welcome treat now. This is a good cake for birthdays. If yours is a fat-free diet, this is an answer, too. The first year I worked for the power company as a home service advisor, I was given the recipe by a woman in Fryeburg. She told me it was Mrs. Pike's cake recipe. I never met her, but I have liked using her recipe.

DAFFODIL CAKE

6 eggs, separated
1 ¼ cups sugar
1 cup sifted cake flour
½ teaspoon cream of tartar
½ teaspoon vanilla

¼ teaspoon almond
   flavoring
½ teaspoon lemon extract
½ teaspoon baking powder
½ teaspoon salt
2 tablespoons cold water

WHITE PART. 6 egg whites, beaten foamy. Add ¼ teaspoon of the salt, the almond flavoring and vanilla. Sprinkle cream of tartar over the foamy whites. Continue to beat until they hold up in peaks. Fold in ¾ cup of the sugar. Fold in ½ cup of the sifted cake flour. Set bowl aside.

YELLOW PART. 6 egg yolks, beaten until light colored and thick. Add 2 tablespoons cold water and lemon extract. Beat well. Beat in remaining ½ cup sugar. Fold in remaining ½ cup sifted cake flour that has been sifted together with the remaining ¼ teaspoon salt and ½ teaspoon baking powder.

Use large angel cake tin. Do not grease it. Alternate white and yellow batter so you have a marbled effect. Bake at 325 degrees for 60 to 70 minutes.

Invert pan and allow cake to cool 1 hour before removing it.

LUSCIOUS LEMON LAYER CAKE

½ cup shortening
¼ teaspoon salt
1 teaspoon vanilla
1 teaspoon lemon extract
1 cup sugar
1 cup sour milk or buttermilk

2 eggs
2 cups sifted cake flour or
1 and ¾ cups sifted all-purpose flour
¾ teaspoon soda
1 teaspoon baking powder

Cream shortening. Add salt, extracts and sugar, gradually. Add the eggs one at a time, beating well after each addition. Sift dry ingredients together. Add alternately to creamed mixture with sour milk or buttermilk.

Bake in two 8-inch layer cake pans that have been greased and floured. If you have square pans, the cake cuts to better advantage. Bake at 350 degrees for 25 minutes.

Cool and fill with . . .

LEMON FILLING

Mix ½ cup sugar, 2 tablespoons flour, ¾ cup cold water. Add pinch of salt. Add grated rind of 1 lemon. Cook until thick, using a low heat. Add 1 beaten egg yolk and juice of 1 lemon, 2 tablespoons butter. Cook 2 minutes more. Cool and fill cake.

Use 1 egg white for . . .

RELIABLE ICING

1 egg white	3 tablespoons cold water
⅞ cup sugar	1 tablespoon white
Pinch of salt	corn syrup
Pinch of cream of tartar	1 teaspoon vanilla

Stir all together in top of double boiler. Allow to stand for ½ hour. This makes a smoother 7-minute frosting. Set over boiling water and start beating. If you use a mixer, this takes 4 minutes. A hand beater requires 7 minutes. Remove from heat. Beat with a spoon for a minute. Ice top of layer cake.

★Cakes that show off Maine apples and Maine blueberries are very popular. This sliced apple cake is one of my favorites, and the blueberry cake is my next-to-favorite in this kind of cake. It is more a coffee cake type blueberry cake than my favorite melt-in-your-mouth blueberry cake that appears in Cooking Down East.

SLICED APPLE CAKE

1 cup cooking oil	1 teaspoon cinnamon
1 and 1/3 cups sugar	1 teaspoon salt
1 teaspoon vanilla	1 heaping cup thinly
3 eggs	sliced apples
2 cups sifted flour	1 cup chopped nuts
1 teaspoon soda	

Beat oil, sugar and vanilla together; add 3 eggs one at a time, beating well after each addition. Sift dry ingredients together and add to creamed mixture. Fold in thinly sliced apples and chopped nuts. You may cut down on the amount of nuts and increase the apple slices if you prefer. Turn into greased, large angel cake pan. Mix 2 tablespoons sugar with ½ teaspoon cinnamon and sprinkle over top of batter. Bake at 350 degrees for 50 minutes.

BLUEBERRY CAKE

3 cups sifted flour
2 cups sugar
3 teaspoons baking powder
1 teaspoon salt
2 eggs
1 cup milk

1/3 cup cooking oil
½ teaspoon vanilla
2 cups Maine blueberries

Sift dry ingredients together into a large mixing bowl. Add eggs, milk, oil and vanilla and beat vigorously for about 2 minutes. Fold in with loving care the 2 cups blueberries. Turn batter into greased and floured 9 x 13-inch pan. Combine ¾ teaspoon nutmeg with ½ cup sugar, sprinkle over top of batter. Bake at 350 degrees for 50 minutes. Serve warm. This cake freezes well.

★When I used this carrot cake with its cream cheese frosting recipe in a special article for Thanksgiving, it was called Recipes for Remembrance. I like that and remembering the friend from Dexter who sent this recipe to me. She and her husband will long be remembered, for they established scholarships to help young people in that part of Maine, and that is good to think about.

CARROT CAKE

4 eggs, separated
2 cups sugar
1½ cups cooking oil
2 cups sifted flour
2 teaspoons soda

2 teaspoons cinnamon
¼ teaspoon salt
3 cups grated carrots
1 teaspoon vanilla

Beat the egg whites until they hold up in peaks. Add about ¼ cup of the sugar to these so they will hold up until ready to be folded into the batter.

Cream together the remaining sugar, oil and egg yolks, beating until light and creamy.

Sift dry ingredients together and add slowly to creamed mixture. Fold in grated carrots, beaten egg whites and vanilla. Turn into 2 greased and floured 8-inch layer cake pans or into a large angel cake pan that has been greased. Either way, bake cake at 350 degrees for 1 hour. Frost with . . .

CREAM CHEESE FROSTING

½ stick margarine
3-ounce package
    cream cheese
½ a pound box
    confectioners' sugar

½ cup chopped nuts
½ teaspoon vanilla

Cream margarine, softened cream cheese and confectioners' sugar. Add chopped nuts and vanilla. Frost cake when cooled, or fill and frost layers of cake.

★Everyone has a favorite chocolate cake recipe. This one happens to be mine. I've been scolded several times because it did not appear in Cooking Down East. It is a comfortable feeling to know I have a second chance.

LOVELIGHT CHOCOLATE CAKE

2 eggs, separated
1½ cups sugar
2 squares chocolate,
    melted
1 and 2/3 cups sifted flour

¾ teaspoon soda
¾ teaspoon salt
1/3 cup cooking oil
1 cup buttermilk
1 teaspoon vanilla

Melt chocolate, allow to cool slightly before adding to batter. Beat the egg whites until they hold up in shape, then add ½ cup of the sugar to beaten whites and set aside.

Sift flour, measure and sift together with remaining sugar, soda and salt into a large bowl. Add oil and ½ cup of the buttermilk to the dry ingredients. Use mixer and beat at low speed for 1 minute. Add remaining buttermilk, the unbeaten egg yolks, the cooled chocolate and the vanilla. Beat 1 minute at medium speed. Fold in the beaten egg whites and sugar mixture. Turn batter into a greased and lightly flour 9 x 9-inch pan. Bake 1 hour at 350 degrees. Place pan on rack to cool for about 5 minutes, then turn cake onto rack to complete cooling.

Something amazing is always happening and this is one of the times. Not long ago, a new recipe for chocolate cake came my way. I made it, found it just the kind we like, used the recipe in my column. And guess what. In a folder marked "chocolate cakes" to use in this book, I learned these two recipes are almost identical. The new recipe called for 1 and 1/3 cup sifted flour and 1 cup of regular milk. Used either way, it is an excellent cake. Try icing it with this frosting . . .

WHITE MOUNTAIN ICING

1 cup sugar	1 egg white,
1/3 cup water	stiffly beaten
Pinch of salt	½ teaspoon vanilla

Cook sugar and water together in a saucepan, stirring until sugar dissolves. Then cook without stirring, using a medium heat, until syrup will form a thread when dropped from the tip of a spoon. Remove from heat and pour in a thin stream over the stiffly beaten egg white, to which salt has been added. Add vanilla and continue beating with electric mixer until it reaches the right consistency to spread. Frost only the top of cake. If you wish, melt 1 square cooking chocolate, add about ½ teaspoon margarine to make it appear glossy, and dribble this melted mixture all over top of frosting. Do this just before frosting "sets." Allow to harden before cutting.

CHOCOLATE
POUND CAKE

2 sticks margarine	¼ teaspoon almond extract
1/3 cup vegetable	2½ cups sifted flour
shortening	½ cup cocoa
½ teaspoon salt	1 cup milk
3 cups sugar	1 teaspoon baking powder
5 eggs	
2 tablespoons vanilla	

This is rather an unusual cake — not only in the ingredients called for but in the mixing directions.

Cream margarine and vegetable shortening together, add salt. Add sugar, gradually. Do not be alarmed at the amount, for the cake has no icing, since it is a pound cake. Add eggs one at a time, beating well after each addition. Add flavoring. Yes, the amount of vanilla is correct.

Sift flour, measure and sift together with cocoa. Add to creamed mixture alternately with milk. Before adding the very last of flour and cocoa mixture, add the baking powder to it, then add to cake mixture. You thought I had forgotten the baking powder, didn't you? See what I mean by unusual?

Mix batter thoroughly. Pour into well-greased large-size angel cake pan. The pan will be chock full when cake is baked. Bake at 325 degrees for 1 hour and 25 minutes. Do not open oven door while it bakes. Place pan on rack to cool before removing cake. Makes 20 servings. Freezes well.

CHOCOLATE CHIP CAKE

1½ cups cut-up dates
1¼ cups cold water
Bring to boil in saucepan, mix well, set aside to cool
1½ sticks margarine
1 cup sugar
½ teaspoon salt
1 teaspoon vanilla

2 eggs
2 cups sifted flour
1 teaspoon soda
1 heaping tablespoon cocoa
TOPPING
½ cup sugar
One 6-ounce package chocolate bits
½ cup chopped nuts

Cream shortening. Add sugar gradually, add salt and vanilla. Add eggs one at a time, beating well after each addition. Sift flour, soda and cocoa together. Add alternately to creamed mixture with the date mixture that has cooled. Turn into greased 9 x 13-inch pan. Sprinkle sugar evenly over top of batter. Distribute chocolate bits and nuts over top. Bake at 350 degrees for 35 minutes. Cool in pan, cut in small squares, remove from pan. This freezes well.

★Spumoni cake comes from North Anson; this is a heritage recipe. Imagine the delight of the person who shared her family recipe to learn that a South Portland woman used it and now, at holiday time, she makes them "by the dozen" for her church and to share with her family.

SPUMONI CAKE

1 stick margarine	2 cups sifted flour
1 cup sugar	2 teaspoons baking powder
1 teaspoon vanilla	½ teaspoon salt
2 eggs	1 cup evaporated milk

Cream shortening, sugar, vanilla and eggs, using mixer if you have one; beat on high speed until light and fluffy. Sift dry ingredients together 3 times, turn into bowl with creamed mixture. Make two or three "wells," turn evaporated milk into the wells. Mix on low speed just enough to blend. Divide batter into 3 parts.

1. Add 4 drops green color and 1 cup chopped nuts to one batter.

2. Add 10 diced maraschino cherries and a few drops juice to the second batter.

3. Blend 2 tablespoons milk with 1 tablespoon cocoa and add to third batter.

Grease and flour a 9 x 5 x 3-inch loaf pan, spoon batter into prepared pan in 1, 2, 3 order. Bake 1 hour at 325 degrees. Cool, wrap and store in a cool place and allow to ripen.

This cake is placed on a board and sliced thin, to show off its marbled effect. Spumoni cake is reminiscent of what our mothers used to make and yet it is as up-to-date as any cake we might choose.

★Cake recipes in Maine have always had interesting names, like Bangor cake, Taylor cake, eagle cake. And then there is Roxbury cake. These cakes are apt to be of a coarser grain texture. Usually these contain spices, molasses and raisins. Often baked in a bread-tin type pan, they need no icing and are sliced for serving.

ROXBURY CAKE

2 eggs
½ cup sugar
½ cup molasses
¼ teaspoon salt
¼ cup shortening, melted
1 teaspoon vanilla

1½ cups sifted flour
1 teaspoon soda
½ teaspoon cinnamon
½ teaspoon nutmeg
½ cup sour milk or
    buttermilk
½ cup seedless raisins
½ cup chopped nuts

Beat 2 eggs until they are thick and light colored, add sugar, molasses and salt. Add melted shortening, slightly cooled, and vanilla. Sift flour, measure and sift together with soda, cinnamon and nutmeg. You may want to save out a bit of flour to mix with raisins and nuts.

Add sifted dry ingredients alternately to creamed mixture with the sour milk or buttermilk. Fold in floured raisins and nuts. Turn batter into greased and floured 9 x 5 x 3-inch loaf pan. Bake 1 hour at 350 degrees. Turn onto rack to cool, then wrap and store. Slice to serve.

OATMEAL CAKE

1 cup quick cooking
    oatmeal
1¼ cups boiling water
1 stick margarine
1 cup granulated sugar
1 cup brown sugar
½ teaspoon salt

1 teaspoon vanilla
2 eggs
1½ cups sifted flour
1 teaspoon soda
1 teaspoon cinnamon
½ teaspoon nutmeg

Pour boiling water over the quick cooking oatmeal and let stand ½ hour. Cream margarine, add salt and vanilla. Add both sugars, gradually. Add 2 eggs one at a time, beating well after each addition. Sift dry ingredients and add alternately with oatmeal mixture to the creamed mixture.

Turn into well-greased 13 x 9 x 2-inch pan. Bake at 350 degrees for about 50 minutes or until cake tests done. Place pan on cake rack and spread following topping on cake, then place pan back in oven under broiler. If you do not have a broiler, you could spread topping on cake, then put it back in oven, still at 350 degrees, for about 10 minutes.

OATMEAL CAKE
TOPPING

1 stick margarine
1 cup brown sugar
¼ cup milk
1 cup flaked cocoanut

½ cup chopped nuts
¼ teaspoon salt
1 teaspoon vanilla

Cream margarine. Add salt and vanilla. Stir in sugar, add milk and cocoanut. Nuts may be added now or sprinkled on top once frosting has been spread on top of cake. Turn on broiler, place pan of baked cake and topping under broiler. Watch closely as this would burn easily. Toast until golden brown. Cool, cut into squares for serving. Serves 16 to 20.

PRUNE CAKE

1½ cups sugar
1 cup cooking oil
3 eggs
1 cup cooked prunes, pitted
   and mashed or chopped
1 cup buttermilk
½ teaspoon salt
1 teaspoon vanilla

2 cups sifted flour
1 teaspoon soda
½ teaspoon cinnamon
½ teaspoon allspice
½ teaspoon nutmeg
½ teaspoon powdered
   cloves
1 cup chopped nuts

Blend the sugar, oil and eggs until mixture is light colored. Sift all dry ingredients together. Add alternately to first mixture with buttermilk. Stir in the vanilla, prunes and chopped nuts. Turn into well-greased 9 x 13-inch pan. Bake at 350 degrees for 50 minutes. While cake is still warm in pan make holes in top of cake, using a toothpick, and pour following frosting over warm cake . . .

BUTTERMILK FROSTING

1 cup sugar
½ cup buttermilk
1 stick margarine
Pinch of salt

1 tablespoon white
   corn syrup
½ teaspoon soda
1 teaspoon vanilla

Combine all ingredients in a saucepan and bring to a boil. Remove from heat and pour over the warm cake. This will serve 16 to 20.

★Gradually, these cake recipes have been leading up to the fruit cakes we make at holiday time. Choosing the recipes from all that have appeared in my column was not an easy task — there have been so many. After all, the selection that appeared in Cooking Down East covered a wide range, but you will like these as well.

Victorian applesauce cake may sound old fashioned but the method of mixing is strictly up-to-date. The number of cakes you will make from this recipe will depend upon the size pans you use.

VICTORIAN APPLESAUCE CAKE

2 cups sifted flour
1½ cups sugar
1½ teaspoons soda
1½ teaspoons salt
2 tablespoons cocoa
½ teaspoon cinnamon
½ teaspoon powdered
   cloves
½ teaspoon nutmeg
½ teaspoon allspice
½ cup vegetable
   shortening
2 eggs, unbeaten
1½ cups unsweetened
   applesauce
¾ cup diced mixed
   candied fruit
¾ cup diced dates

Sift dry ingredients together into a large bowl. Add vegetable shortening and three-quarters cup of the applesauce. Beat 150 strokes by hand or, if using an electric mixer, beat for 1½ minutes using low speed.

Add remaining three-quarters cup applesauce and the 2 unbeaten eggs. Beat 2½ minutes. Fold in the fruit and dates, not floured. Turn into two well-greased loaf pans, size 9 x 5 inches, or use smaller pans, divide batter and fill pans to about two-thirds full.

Sprinkle tops of batter in pans with topping made of the following: two tablespoons sugar mixed with ¼ cup chopped nuts. Bake 1 hour at 350 degrees. Cool on rack and store as for any fruit cake.

MIRACLE DARK FRUIT CAKE

One 8-ounce package dates
One package seedless
  raisins
2/3 cup margarine

1 ¼ cups brown sugar
¼ cup molasses
1 ½ cups hot water

Combine ingredients in a saucepan. Bring to boil, boil gently for 3 minutes.

Turn hot mixture into large mixing bowl, then allow to cool. Beat in:

10 eggs, one at a time
½ cup brandy
1 pound mixed
  candied fruit

1 package currants
2 packages seedless raisins
2 cups cut-up walnuts

Packages of raisins might vary in size from 12 to 16 ounces. Currants will probably be in an 11-ounce package. This makes no difference. Once all the fruit has been mixed in, then the following dry ingredients are sifted together and added:

3 cups sifted flour
2 teaspoons cinnamon
½ teaspoon nutmeg

1 teaspoon soda
1 teaspoon baking powder
1 teaspoon salt

Prepare four 9 x 5-inch pans. Turn fruit cake batter into four pans, dividing evenly. Bake 1½ to 2 hours at 275 degrees. Test for doneness, using a cake tester or a toothpick. Turn cakes onto racks to cool. Glaze tops of cakes with equal amounts of water and white corn syrup that have been boiled vigorously in a saucepan for one minute, then flavored with brandy.

This recipe may be halved. It is a delicious dark fruit cake. Wrap and store as you would any fruit cake. There are three pounds of raisins used in this recipe.

MRS. MILLER'S FRUIT CAKE

1½ cups butter or
  margarine
1½ cups sugar
6 eggs, beaten until light
½ cup milk
3 cups sifted flour

1½ teaspoons
  baking powder
½ teaspoon salt
1 pound golden raisins
¼ pound walnuts, broken
3 tablespoons finely
  diced citron

Cream shortening, adding sugar gradually. Add beaten eggs and continue beating until mixture is light and fluffy. Sift flour and measure. Reserve a small amount to mix with raisins, walnuts (which are not chopped, merely broken), and diced citron. Sift remainder of flour with baking powder and salt. Add sifted dry ingredients alternately with milk to creamed mixture. Fold in floured nuts, raisins and citron. Use two well-greased 9 x 5-inch loaf pans, turn batter into pans, bake at 325 degrees for 1½ hours. Place pans on rack to cool, remove cakes, wrap and store.

WHITE FRUIT CAKE

1 cup butter	One pound each
2 cups sugar	golden raisins
1 teaspoon salt	pitted dates, cut small
1 tablespoon vanilla	walnuts, broken
Whites of 7 eggs	½ cup candied lemon peel
1 cup light cream	½ cup candied orange peel
2½ cups sifted flour	4 ounces candied cherries
1 teaspoon soda	1 small package figs
	¼ cup finely-cut citron

Beat 7 egg whites until stiff, add ½ cup of the sugar to these. Set aside. Cream butter, add salt and vanilla and remainder of sugar.

Mix all of chopped fruits and nuts together in a large bowl. Use ½ cup of flour called for in recipe and lightly coat fruit.

Sift remainder of measured flour with soda. Add dry ingredients alternately to creamed mixture with the light cream. Fold in the beaten egg whites and sugar. Combine with lightly-floured fruit and nuts.

Prepare two loaf pans, 9 x 5-inches, by greasing well, then line with brown paper, which you will also grease. Turn batter into pans, spread evenly. Bake one hour at 350 degrees, reduce heat to 325 degrees and bake one hour longer. Turn onto racks to cool. Wrap and store in covered crock or in refrigerator. Freezes well.

In adding fruit and nuts to cakes of this kind, you will not need to cut dates, cherries, and nuts for these cakes are ripened, then sliced thin, and you slice right through the fruit and nuts anyway.

★There is just no other way to refer to these next three cakes except to call them mixed-up. That is the way the index label reads in my personal cookbook of recipes. That is the one that has all the recipes you have sent me, usually in your handwriting. They are all taped in and I have indexed them to suit my fancy.

EGG NOG CAKE

One package (1 lb. 3 oz.)
   yellow cake mix
One 3-ounce package
   instant vanilla
   pudding mix

1 teaspoon nutmeg
¾ cup cooking oil
¾ cup sherry
4 eggs

Mix dry cake mix, dry instant vanilla pudding mix and nutmeg in larger bowl of electric mixer. Add oil and sherry, beat mixture slowly to mix ingredients. Add 4 unbeaten eggs and beat mixture for 5 minutes so ingredients are well blended. Turn batter into well-greased large-size angel cake pan. Bake at 350 degrees for 50 minutes. Place pan on rack and allow to cool in pan for 10 minutes, then cake may be turned out of pan and the cooling completed. Place in covered container. This cake is better if allowed to mellow for a day or so. It freezes very well.

'SOCK IT TO ME' CAKE

One 16-ounce yellow or
   butter cake mix
½ cup sugar
¾ cup cooking oil

1 cup commercial
   sour cream
2 teaspoons vanilla
4 eggs

Turn cake mix into bowl, add sugar, oil and sour cream, stir to mix, add vanilla. Add 4 eggs one at a time, beating well after each addition. Use a large angel cake pan, well-greased. Turn half of cake batter into pan. Have prepared:

3 tablespoons brown sugar   ½ cup chopped nuts
2 teaspoons cinnamon

Combine and sprinkle this over batter in pan, then turn remaining batter into pan. Bake at 325 degrees for one hour. Place pan on rack to cool for 10 minutes. Remove cake from pan to cool and ice with:

1 cup confectioners' sugar   2 teaspoons milk
2 tablespoons melted butter

Mix ingredients and ice top of cake. This cake serves 16.

★Although I am a strictly "from scratch" person, I still think these mixed-up cakes are excellent. They are like pound cakes and are rarely iced. Pistachio cake fits into many of the holidays during the year, when you want a pale green cake; and if almond happens to be your favorite flavor, then you will make one of these cakes just any old time.

PISTACHIO CAKE

One package almond cake mix (Only available in A & P brand) or use white cake mix
One 3-ounce package pistachio instant pudding mix (Royal brand, only)

¾ cup cold water, add a bit of green food coloring
¾ cup cooking oil
4 eggs
1 teaspoon almond extract

Stir almond or white cake mix together with the dry pistachio instant pudding mix. Add some green food coloring to cold water. Stir water and oil into mixed dry ingredients. Add almond extract. Add eggs one at a time, beating well at low speed. After combining ingredients, increase speed of mixer and continue to beat for five minutes. Grease a large angel cake pan, turn batter into pan and bake at 350 degrees for about 50 minutes. Place pan on rack to cool for 10 minutes, remove cake from pan and cool. Store in covered container. This cake freezes well.

COOKIES AND BARS

★You could hardly believe the many kinds of hermit cookie recipes that are used by Maine cooks. You see, husbands enter into all hermit recipe discussions. It is said that as we grow older we are bemused by memory. That is why men remember their mother's hermits. Only, sometimes they remember rolled hermits when really they were a drop cookie. Some mothers used molasses, others used only white sugar. Some added nuts as well as raisins, other mothers would not think of adding nuts. Some used sweet milk, others used sour. Some day, if you want to start a discussion, just ask, "What kind of hermits did your mother use to make?"

For sentimental reasons, I am using a hermit recipe as the first in this section on cookies and bars. It is because the first cookie recipe in my other cookbook was for old-fashioned hermits. This time, it is a whole new hermit recipe and it is called that—New Hermits.

NEW HERMITS

1 cup evaporated milk
1 tablespoon vinegar
½ cup shortening
2 cups brown sugar, well-packed
½ teaspoon salt
2 eggs
½ teaspoon vanilla

2 cups sifted flour
1 teaspoon soda
1 teaspoon cinnamon
1 teaspoon powdered cloves
1 teaspoon allspice
¼ teaspoon nutmeg
3 cups or 1 pound seedless raisins
½ cup chopped nuts

Mix milk and vinegar together and let stand. Cream shortening, add sugar gradually, add salt and vanilla. Add eggs one at a time, beating well after each addition. Sift dry ingredients together and add to creamed mixture with evaporated milk mixture. Stir in raisins and chopped nuts. Drop by teaspoonfuls onto greased cookie sheets. Bake at 350 degrees about 15 minutes. Makes about 6 dozen cookies.

★This interesting recipe for honey drops came to me from Fort Kent. It is easy to make and, interestingly enough, once the cookies are baked and slightly cooled they are put together with apricot jam. So, depending upon whether you want tea-size cookies or lunch-size, you will vary the amount of dough you drop from a teaspoon onto your cookie sheet.

HONEY DROPS

2 sticks margarine	3½ cups sifted flour
1 cup brown sugar, firmly packed	2 teaspoons soda
	½ teaspoon salt
2 eggs	1 teaspoon vanilla
6 tablespoons honey	Jar of apricot jam or preserves

Cream shortening, add brown sugar gradually. Add 2 eggs and beat well. Stir in the honey and vanilla. Sift dry ingredients together, add to creamed mixture. Chill dough several hours or overnight. Form dough into balls, using about 1 teaspoon dough for each. Place balls of dough on ungreased cookie sheets. Bake at 350 degrees for 10 to 12 minutes until golden brown on top and the cookies spring back when lightly touched.

Cool cookies slightly. Put together in pairs with apricot jam between. Of course this means two bottoms together.

OLD FASHIONED
THIN SUGAR COOKIES

2 sticks margarine	2 cups sifted flour
1 cup sugar	½ teaspoon soda
1 egg	½ teaspoon cream of tartar
2 teaspoons vanilla	¼ teaspoon salt

Cream shortening, add sugar, egg and vanilla and mix until light and creamy. Sift flour, soda, cream of tartar and salt together. This is a correct proportion of soda and cream of tartar. Again, there is no liquid in this recipe because of the two sticks of margarine.

Chill dough. Roll into small balls. Use greased pan, press balls down, using fresh dish towel over end of glass, dipped in water. Some cooks dip end of glass in flour; either way this makes for thin cookies, without rolling the dough.

Bake at 375 degrees for 8 to 10 minutes or until cookies are brown around the edges. These are delightful cookies.

JUMBO MOLASSES COOKIES

1 cup melted shortening
1 cup sugar
1 cup molasses
1 egg
5 1/4 cups sifted flour
1 1/2 teaspoons cream of tartar
1 1/2 teaspoons ginger

1 1/2 teaspoons cinnamon
1/2 teaspoon cloves
1/2 teaspoon salt
2/3 cup boiling water
3 1/2 teaspoons soda
2 teaspoons vanilla

Combine the melted shortening and sugar, add molasses, then the egg, and beat until creamy.

Dissolve soda in boiling water, add to molasses mixture. Add dry ingredients that have been sifted together. Add vanilla and mix well. This will be a soft dough but it is to be chilled overnight or for several hours, then it becomes firm and is exactly right for rolling.

This depends on whether or not you like to roll cookie dough. If you do, roll to one-eighth inch thickness. Using a 3-inch cookie cutter, place rounds of dough on greased cookie sheets. Far easier will be to make large balls (about 1 1/4 inches) and place on cookie sheets. Use fresh dish towel drawn over a glass, dampen and press down balls of dough.

Bake at 400 degrees for 8 to 10 minutes. Remove at once from pans to racks for cooling. This will make 75 great big cookies. This dough is perfection to work with.

OLD-FASHIONED DROP MOLASSES COOKIES

1/2 cup shortening, melted
1/2 cup sugar
1/2 cup molasses
1 egg
1/2 cup sour milk or buttermilk or 1 teaspoon vinegar in 1/2 cup sweet milk

2 1/2 cups sifted flour
1/2 teaspoon salt
1/2 teaspoon ginger
1/2 teaspoon cinnamon
1/2 teaspoon powdered cloves
1 and 3/4 teaspoon soda

Cream melted shortening, sugar and molasses, add unbeaten egg and beat until light and creamy. Sift dry ingredients together and add alternately to creamed mixture with the ½ cup sour milk. Using teaspoons, drop cookie dough onto greased cookie sheets. Bake at 375 degrees for 10 to 12 minutes. Remove cookies from pans, cool on racks and store in covered container. Makes about 5 dozen cookies.

★This is an old-fashioned drop cookie recipe. It is easy to make and has delicious flavor. If you recall the Green Farm between Stratton and Rangeley, then you will be interested that this recipe came from there.

ELEPHANT'S EARS

1 stick margarine
½ teaspoon salt
1 teaspoon vanilla
1 cup sugar
2 tablespoons molasses
1 egg

1 teaspoon soda, dissolved in ½ cup sour milk or buttermilk
2½ cups sifted flour
½ cup seedless raisins
¼ cup chopped nuts

Cream shortening, add salt and vanilla. Add sugar gradually, then the molasses. Add unbeaten egg and beat until light and creamy. Add soda to sour milk (keep in mind you can sour sweet milk by adding 1 teaspoon vinegar to ½ cup), stir. Add sifted flour and sour milk alternately to creamed mixture. Fold in raisins and nuts, using all raisins if you prefer.

Drop by teaspoonfuls onto greased cookie sheets. Bake at 375 degrees for 12 to 15 minutes. Makes 4 dozen cookies.

BEST OATMEAL COOKIES

2 sticks margarine
1 cup granulated sugar
½ cup brown sugar
1 egg
1 teaspoon vanilla
½ teaspoon salt

1½ cups sifted flour
1 teaspoon soda
1 teaspoon cinnamon
1½ cups oatmeal, uncooked
½ cup seedless raisins

Cream margarine, add salt and vanilla. Add two kinds of sugar, gradually. Add unbeaten egg and beat until light and creamy. There is no liquid in this recipe. Sift dry ingredients together and add to the creamed mixture. Fold in the uncooked oatmeal. Fold in raisins. Drop by spoonfuls onto greased cookie sheets. Bake at 350 degrees for 10 minutes.

CARROT COOKIES
with
ORANGE ICING

¾ cups shortening
1 teaspoon salt
½ teaspoon vanilla
¾ cup sugar
1 egg

2 cups sifted flour
2 teaspoons baking powder
¾ cup cooked,
    mashed carrots

Cream shortening, salt and vanilla. The large amount of salt is used since none is added to carrots. Add sugar, gradually. Add egg and beat until light and fluffy. Sift flour and baking powder together. Pare and cook carrots in amount to make ¾ cup when mashed. Fold in mashed carrots. Drop by spoonfuls onto greased cookie sheet. Bake at 350 degrees for 10 to 12 minutes. Makes about 40 cookies. While still slightly warm, frost with following:

ORANGE ICING

1 tablespoon margarine
1½ tablespoons
    orange juice
1 tablespoon grated
    orange rind

½ teaspoon almond extract
Enough confectioners'
    sugar to spread easily

Mix ingredients together until creamy and frost carrot cookies.

ORIGINAL
TOLL HOUSE COOKIES

1 stick margarine
½ cup light brown sugar,
    firmly packed
½ cup granulated sugar
1 teaspoon vanilla
¼ teaspoon salt
1 egg

1½ cups sifted flour
2 tablespoons hot water
½ teaspoon soda, dissolved
    in the hot water
1 cup chocolate bits
½ cup chopped nuts

These cookies were originated at the celebrated Toll House in Whitman, Massachusetts, by Ruth Wakefield. Soon they became popular all over the country. Although you will find the recipe for these cookies on the package of chocolate bits, stating it is the original recipe, it is not this recipe. This is the one that was printed on a long-ago package and it is the original recipe—really. Toll House cookies should be crispy and brown all through.

Cream margarine, add salt and vanilla. Add two kinds of sugar, gradually. Add unbeaten egg and beat all together until mixture is light and creamy.

Dissolve soda in hot water, sift and measure flour, and add these two mixtures alternately to creamed mixture. Fold in chocolate bits and nuts. Drop by teaspoon onto greased cookie sheets. This will make 50 drop cookies of about 2-inch size.

Bake at 375 degrees for 10 to 12 minutes.

COWBOY COOKIES

2 sticks margarine
1 cup granulated sugar
1 cup brown sugar,
    firmly packed
1 teaspoon vanilla
2 eggs

2 cups sifted flour
1 teaspoon soda
½ teaspoon baking powder
½ teaspoon salt
2 cups uncooked oatmeal
1 cup chocolate bits
    or raisins

Cream shortening, and vanilla, add sugars gradually, beat until smooth and creamy. Add eggs one at a time, beating well after each addition. Beat until light and creamy.

Sift dry ingredients together. Add flour mixture to creamed mixture. Stir in the uncooked oatmeal—this will be a crumbly mixture. Fold in chocolate bits or raisins. Drop by teaspoonfuls onto greased cookie sheets. Bake at 350 degrees for 10 to 12 minutes. Makes about 7 dozen cookies.

BANANA NUGGETS

1½ cups sifted flour	¾ cup shortening
1 cup sugar	1 egg, well beaten
1 teaspoon soda	1 cup mashed bananas
1 teaspoon nutmeg	1 and ¾ cups
¾ teaspoon cinnamon	uncooked oatmeal
1 teaspoon salt	1 cup chocolate bits or
	seedless raisins

Sift together flour, sugar, soda, salt, nutmeg, and cinnamon into a mixing bowl. Cut in the shortening (can use 1½ sticks margarine), using a pastry blender or two knives, making mixture like meal. Add well-beaten egg, mashed bananas, uncooked oatmeal, and fold in chocolate bits, although raisins are better. Drop by spoonfuls onto ungreased cookie sheets. Bake at 350 degrees for 15 minutes. Makes about 48 cookies.

★We use apples in many ways in our recipes in Maine, Probably one of the best ways is to use applesauce in this drop sugar cookie recipe.

APPLESAUCE COOKIES

1 stick margarine	2 cups sifted flour
1 cup sugar	½ teaspoon salt
1 egg, well beaten	½ teaspoon cinnamon
1 cup applesauce	½ teaspoon nutmeg
1 teaspoon soda	½ teaspoon powdered
	cloves
	1 cup seedless raisins

Cream shortening, add sugar gradually, beat until light. Stir soda into applesauce, combine with creamed mixture along with the well-beaten egg. Sift dry ingredients together, add to creamed mixture. Fold in seedless raisins, adding chopped nuts too, if you wish.

Drop by teaspoonfuls onto greased cookie sheets, allowing plenty of space between them. Bake at 375 degrees about 15 minutes. Makes about 4 dozen cookies.

★Meringue-type cookies are very popular and if you wanted them to stay up all night, then you would call them by that name. I decided it was far more interesting than just plain meringue cookies.

STAY-UP-ALL-NIGHT COOKIES

Beat 2 egg whites, that are at room temperature, until they hold up in peaks
Add 2/3 cup sugar, gradually

Add ½ teaspoon vanilla, beat until mixture is very stiff
Fold in 1 cup chocolate bits

Before you start to mix cookies, turn oven switch on and set temperature to 375 degrees.

After mixing meringue cookies, drop mixture by teaspoonfuls onto ungreased cookie sheet. Put pan of cookies into oven, close oven door, turn oven switch to OFF. Leave pan of cookies in oven overnight. Makes 30 cookies.

PEANUT BUTTER MACAROONS

2 egg whites, room temperature
¼ teaspoon salt

¾ cup sugar
½ cup creamy peanut butter

Beat egg whites with salt until frothy. Add sugar gradually, beating until stiff peaks form. Fold in peanut butter. Spread piece of foil on a cookie sheet—it needs no greasing. Drop mixture one inch apart on foil, using teaspoon. Bake at 325 degrees for 20 minutes. Makes 40 cookies. When cool, they will peel right off foil.

CHOCOLATE MACAROONS

1 cup chocolate bits (One 6-ounce package)
2 egg whites
½ cup sugar

¼ teaspoon salt
1 teaspoon vanilla
2/3 cup flaked cocoanut
½ cup chopped nuts

Melt chocolate bits slowly. Beat egg whites until they are stiff but not dry, then add sugar, gradually. Add melted chocolate, then vanilla, salt, cocoanut and chopped nuts.

Drop by teaspoons on greased cookie sheet. Makes 30 cookies. Bake at 350 degrees for 15 to 18 minutes.

★The fact you use colored miniature marshmallows in making these unbaked cookies gives them the name cathedral cookies. They are good any time of year, but at holiday time they have deeper meaning since you can almost see the stained glass of church windows as you slice the cookies. I shall always like to remember Pam, who was our paper delivery girl and who came to have her picture taken for the Sunday paper, as she made these cookies in our kitchen.

CATHEDRAL COOKIES

2 tablespoons margarine
Melt with:
One 12-ounce package
    chocolate bits
Cool, then stir gently
Add:
1 egg, beaten
½ teaspoon salt

Fold-in:
3 cups colored miniature
    marshmallows
½ cup chopped nuts
When all is mixed, mold
    into rolls
Turn or shake flaked
    cocoanut onto a board
    and coat rolls completely
    with cocoanut

After rolling in cocoanut, wrap in plastic wrap or foil. Place in refrigerator or freezer for several hours. When ready to use, slice in desired width.

DOUBLE BATCH BROWNIES

4 squares unsweetened
    chocolate
4 eggs
2 cups sugar
1 cup cooking oil

1 teaspoon salt
1 tablespoon vanilla
1 cup sifted flour,
    slightly rounded
1 cup coarsely
    chopped nuts

Melt chocolate over very low heat, cool slightly. Beat eggs until thick and light colored. Add sugar gradually, then oil, continuing to beat. Add salt, vanilla and cooled chocolate Fold in the cup of sifted flour and chopped nuts.

Turn into buttered 9 x 13-inch pan. Bake at 350 degrees for 30 minutes.

Place pan on rack to cool. Cut into squares. Store or freeze.

QUICK APPLE DANISH

Mix as for pie crust:	1 cup shortening
2 cups sifted flour	1 egg yolk, slightly beaten,
1 tablespoon sugar	enough milk added to
1 teaspoon salt	make 2/3 cup in all

Sift flour, sugar and salt together into bowl. Cut in shortening, using pastry blender or two knives. Using fork, beat egg yolk in cup, add enough milk to make two-thirds cup in all. Mix lightly with dry ingredients. Divide in half. Roll out to fit onto a cookie sheet. Cover this pastry with one cup crushed corn flakes, then a thick layer of thinly sliced apples.

Mix 1 cup sugar with 1 teaspoon cinnamon. Spread all over apple slices. Roll remaining dough, place on top, press edges together and flute these to give a neat appearance. Using a table fork, prick top pastry in several places. Beat egg white stiff and spread all over top. Bake at 350 degrees for 40 minutes. Place pan on rack to cool.

While still hot, mix 1 cup confectioners' sugar with enough lemon juice to make runny icing and dribble all over top crust. Cool, cut in squares or bars.

BAKED APPLE SQUARES

1 and ¾ cups sugar	1 teaspoon vanilla
3 eggs	1 cup cooking oil
2 cups sifted flour	2 cups thinly sliced
1 teaspoon baking powder	McIntosh apples
1 teaspoon cinnamon	1 cup chopped nuts
½ teaspoon salt	(optional)

Beat sugar and eggs until light colored. Add sifted dry ingredients. Add oil and vanilla. Fold in thinly sliced apples and chopped nuts. Bake in greased 9 x 13-inch pan at 350 degrees for 40 minutes. Place pan on rack to cool, cut in squares. May be frozen.

COFFEE SQUARES

1 stick margarine	½ teaspoon salt
1½ cups brown sugar	1 teaspoon vanilla
1 egg	½ cup warm coffee
1½ cups sifted flour	½ cup butterscotch bits
½ teaspoon soda	¼ cup chopped nuts

Cream shortening, add brown sugar, add egg and beat until light and creamy. Sift dry ingredients together and add to creamed mixture alternately with warm coffee. Spread batter in greased 7 x 11-inch pan. Sprinkle butterscotch bits and nuts over top of batter. Bake at 350 degrees for 35 minutes. Place pan on rack to cool. Cut in squares.

★This recipe for pistachio bars just about tops the list in popularity of bar recipes that have appeared in my column. It came to me from Portland and it is a wonderful recipe. It has nothing to do with the recipe for pistachio cake. Wait until you try these bars and learn the surprise in store. People think of pistachio nuts.

PISTACHIO BARS

3 egg whites	2½ teaspoons baking
1/3 cup sugar	powder
¼ cup shortening	½ teaspoon salt
1 cup sugar	1 cup milk
2 cups sifted cake flour or	1 teaspoon almond extract
1 and ¾ cups sifted	Few drops green
all-purpose flour	food coloring
	1½ squares unsweetened
	chocolate, shaved

Beat egg whites until stiff and add one-third cup sugar. Set aside. Cream shortening, add salt and almond flavoring. Add sugar gradually, mixing until creamy. Sift flour and baking powder together. Add alternately with milk to creamed mixture.

Add green food coloring to batter, taking care not to get it too green. Fold in one square of chocolate that has been shaved, using a paring knife. It will be easier to do this if you place the chocolate in the refrigerator to chill beforehand.

Fold in the beaten egg whites and sugar. Grease and flour a jelly roll pan, about 14 x 10 inches in size. Or use 9 x 13-inch pan, which will give you thicker bars. Or how about using two 6 x 9-inch pans? Bake at 350 degrees about 35 minutes.

Place pan on rack to cool. Frost with a pale tinted green butter frosting. Sprinkle shaved chocolate all over top of frosting. When frosting is hard, cut into about 36 bars.

GRAHAM CRACKER SQUARES

This recipe is not baked and once made needs refrigeration. Butter a 9 x 13-inch pan. Place graham crackers flat in pan. These are not rolled crumbs. Spread with this cooked filling, slightly cooled:

FILLING

1 egg, beaten	1½ cups rolled graham
1 stick margarine	cracker crumbs
1 cup brown sugar	½ cup chopped nuts
¼ teaspoon salt	½ cup flaked cocoanut
½ cup water	1 teaspoon vanilla

Using a saucepan, melt margarine, add beaten egg, brown sugar, salt and water. Bring to a boil, stirring constantly, so egg will be smooth. Remove from heat, quickly stir in the graham cracker crumbs, nuts and cocoanut. Add vanilla. Turn this warm mixture over graham crackers placed in the pan. Spread evenly.

Place another layer of flat graham crackers all over filling, smoothing up edges to make neat.

Make a confectioners' sugar frosting and frost top. Place pan in refrigerator for storing. A glass pan works the very best for these squares. Cut small for serving, as they are rich. These also freeze well. Use a piece of corrugated cardboard, cover with foil, place bars on this, cover with plastic wrap or foil and store in freezer. Takes up very little space.

BUTTER FROSTING

Melt ¼ cup butter
Add 2 cups confectioners'
  sugar

2 tablespoons milk
Pinch of salt
½ teaspoon vanilla

Combine all ingredients and mix smooth. You may not need to add all of milk; use your judgment and mix it to spreading consistency.

FRUIT PUNCH BARS

2 eggs
1½ cups sugar
One can fruit cocktail,
  undrained (1 lb., 1 oz.)
2½ cups sifted flour

1½ teaspoons soda
½ teaspoon salt
1 teaspoon vanilla
1 cup flaked cocoanut

Beat eggs, add sugar, beat until light and creamy. Add fruit cocktail, undrained. Sift dry ingredients together, add to fruit mixture. Add vanilla. Prepare a 15 x 10 x 1-inch pan by greasing and flouring. Turn batter into pan. Sprinkle top of batter with the flaked cocoanut. Bake at 350 degrees for 25 minutes. Bake slightly longer if all you have is a 9 x 13-inch pan.

Place pan on rack to cool, but while bars are still hot dribble glaze all over top . . .

GLAZE

¾ cup sugar
1 stick margarine
¼ cup evaporated milk

½ teaspoon vanilla
Pinch of salt

Bring all ingredients to boil and cook two minutes. Cool slightly. Dribble over hot baked bars. Cool, cut in squares. Of course if you do not have evaporated milk, then you could use cream or milk.

★For more years than I can recall, she has been signing her letters "Sal." She lives in Rockland. It was Sal who compelled me to always autograph "Happy Cooking" in Cooking Down East, for that is the way she has always signed her letters. One day she signed "Keep Cooking," and so she named this cookbook. This is a favorite recipe of Sal's.

HEATH BAR SQUARES

1 stick margarine
1 cup brown sugar
½ cup white sugar
2 cups sifted flour
¼ teaspoon salt

1 egg, beaten
1 cup buttermilk
1 teaspoon soda
1 teaspoon vanilla
6 Heath bars, crushed

Combine margarine, sugars, flour and salt in a bowl, using a pastry blender and cutting in margarine as for pie crust. Reserve ½ cup of mixture to be used for topping.

Beat egg and add to remaining crumb mixture. Combine soda with buttermilk, add to mixture. Add vanilla and mix thoroughly. Turn into buttered 9 x 13-inch pan. Top with reserved mixture.

Crush Heath bars by placing on wax paper on a cutting board, cover with foil and, with a hammer, lightly tap and crush bars. Sprinkle all over top of batter. Bake at 350 degrees for 30 minutes. Place pan on rack to cool, cut in squares.

PEANUT BUTTER BARS

1/3 cup shortening
½ cup peanut butter
¼ teaspoon salt
1 teaspoon vanilla
1 cup sugar

2 eggs, unbeaten
1 cup sifted flour
1 teaspoon baking powder
1 cup chopped nuts

Cream shortening and peanut butter. Add salt and vanilla. Add sugar gradually, then eggs, beating after each addition. Sift flour and baking powder together and add to creamed mixture. Fold in chopped nuts, which may be eliminated if you use crunchy peanut butter. Turn batter into buttered 7 x 11-inch pan. Bake at 325 degrees about 25 minutes. Place pan on rack to cool. Frost with following:

FROSTING

1 ½ cups confectioners' sugar
2 tablespoons melted butter

2 tablespoons peanut butter
Pinch of salt
½ teaspoon vanilla

Mix all ingredients together, frost bars. When frosting is hardened, cut into bars.

DATE SQUARES

2 cups cut-up dates
1/3 cup boiling water, poured over dates and allowed to stand
1 stick margarine
¾ teaspoon salt
¼ teaspoon cinnamon
¼ teaspoon nutmeg
1 teaspoon vanilla

1 cup sugar
2 eggs
1 cup sifted flour
¼ teaspoon soda
½ cup chopped nuts
Grated rind 1 orange
Orange juice may be substituted in place of boiling water

Cream shortening, salt, cinnamon, nutmeg, vanilla and sugar. Add two eggs, beating after each addition and until mixture is creamy. Sift flour and soda together and add to creamed mixture. Add grated orange rind. For greater flavor, if you prefer, use orange juice or part juice and water (heating it of course) to pour over cut-up dates. Fold in chopped nuts. Turn into greased 9 x 13-inch pan, bake at 350 degrees for about 40 minutes. Place pan on rack to cool, then cut into squares.

You will not find batter too thin if you use both boiling water and the juice from the orange.

★It amazed me not long ago to learn I could make marshmallows. Well, at least it is that kind of a topping. You can, too, if you follow these directions. These are a very special kind of treat.

MARSHMALLOW SQUARES

BOTTOM LAYER

1 stick margarine　　　　2 tablespoons brown sugar
1 cup unsifted flour

Using a pastry blender, combine ingredients and press into a 9 x 13-inch pan that has been greased. Bake at 350 degrees for 10 minutes. Place pan on rack to cool.

TOP LAYER

1 ½ envelopes unflavored　　1 cup sugar
　gelatin (1 ½ tablespoons)　1 cup cold water

Mix together in saucepan and bring to a boil. Lower heat and cook for 10 minutes or until very thick and of a marshmallow consistency. Remove from heat and add:

Pinch of salt　　　　　　1 cup confectioners'
1 teaspoon vanilla　　　　　sugar

Turn into larger bowl of electric mixer, beat 10 minutes or until very thick and of a marshmallow consistency. Then, of all things, add 1 teaspoon baking powder. Spread all over top of baked layer. While moist, sprinkle top with flaked cocoanut or colored sugar or chopped nuts. Allow to become firm, cut in squares.

CHRISTMAS FRUIT SQUARES

1 stick margarine,　　　　Pinch of salt
　softened　　　　　　　2 cups chopped pecans
1 cup brown sugar,　　　　1 cup diced
　firmly packed　　　　　　candied pineapple
2 eggs　　　　　　　　　¼ pound red
1 teaspoon vanilla　　　　　candied cherries
1 cup unsifted flour　　　　¼ pound green
　　　　　　　　　　　　candied cherries

Beat margarine and brown sugar together until very light, add two eggs, continue beating until creamy. Add vanilla and salt. Add unsifted flour that has been measured into cup by spoonfuls.

Butter two 11 x 7 x 2-inch pans. Sprinkle one cup chopped nuts into each pan. Divide batter evenly on nuts and spread around pan. Press the candied pineapple and two kinds of colored candied cherries into top of batter, dividing these evenly.

Bake at 300 degrees for 30 to 40 minutes. Place pans on racks to cool. When just barely warm, cut into squares. Makes 4 dozen. These freeze very well, too, and that is every reason in the world to make these in the fall, for your Christmas cooking.

CONFECTIONS

"The daintiest last, to make the end most sweet."

CHERRY BALLS

1 ½ cups fine
shredded cocoanut
½ cup butter or
margarine

1 ½ cups confectioners'
sugar

Knead these 3 ingredients together, then form a bit around a maraschino cherry that has been drained. Make about the size of a small walnut. Roll balls in fine graham cracker crumbs. Place in a plastic covered container in refrigerator to keep. These will freeze.

CANDIED PEEL

5 medium oranges
6 medium lemons
2 medium grapefruit
8 large tangerines

12 cups water
2 ½ cups sugar
½ cup honey
1 and ¾ cups
boiling water

Wash fruit, wipe and remove peelings. Cut peeling into strips. Boil it in 6 cups of the water for 10 minutes. Drain. Repeat process with remaining 6 cups water. After 10 minutes, drain.

In large saucepan combine 1½ cups sugar, ½ cup honey and the 1 and ¾ cups boiling water. Bring to a boil and boil one minute. Add cooked, drained peel and simmer until almost all the syrup has been absorbed or about 30 minutes. Watch carefully and stir to avoid having it stick.

Drain in colander for 10 minutes. Turn the remaining one cup sugar into a large bowl, toss the pieces of fruit peel in this sugar. Spread candied peel on waxed paper to dry. Store in a stone crock.

If you have always wanted to make candied fruit peel, then this is the easy way to do it.

CORNFLAKE HOLLY

1/3 cup margarine	Remove from heat, add
16 large marshmallows	1½ teaspoons green
Melt together in top	food color
double boiler, over	1 teaspoon vanilla
hot water	Add 2½ cups cornflakes

When the cornflakes are added, make certain they are well-coated and not crushed too much. Drop by teaspoons onto waxed paper. If you would like, poke the end of your little finger in center to make tiny wreaths, poke a couple of tiny red cinnamon candies into wreath for decoration. You do not need to do this, for as you drop the holly onto the wax paper it will look like it should and almost ceramic in appearance. It tastes good and will perk up a plate of holiday goodies.

PEANUT BUTTER BALLS

1 cup confectioners' sugar	1 cup peanut butter
1 cup graham cracker	Pinch of salt
crumbs	

Knead these ingredients together. Make into very small balls.

Melt together in top of double boiler over water that is simmering:

One 6-ounce package	One 1½ x 2-inch square
chocolate bits	paraffin, just like you
	use to melt on top
	of jelly

Use toothpick and dip each peanut butter ball into chocolate mixture. Place on wax paper for hardening.

STRAWBERRY DIVINITY FUDGE

3 cups sugar
¾ cup white corn syrup
¾ cup water
Pinch of salt

2 egg whites
One 3-ounce package
    strawberry gelatin
Chopped nuts

Boil sugar, white corn syrup, water and salt in a saucepan until syrup reaches 250 degrees on candy thermometer or if tested in a small amount of cold water it has reached the "crack" stage.

Beat two egg whites stiff and add the dry strawberry gelatin to these. Very slowly add the hot syrup and continue beating until the divinity appears dull. Add nuts. Pour into buttered oblong glass pan. Allow to harden. Cut into 36 pieces. Remember, the day must be clear when you make divinity fudge.

CHOCOLATE CREAM FUDGE

One small can evaporated
    milk (about 6 oz.)
1 and 1/3 cups sugar
¼ teaspoon salt
¼ cup butter or margarine

One 6-ounce package
    chocolate bits
1 cup marshmallow creme
1 teaspoon vanilia
½ cup chopped nuts

Using a saucepan, combine milk, sugar, salt and butter. Bring to a full rolling boil, using a medium heat and stirring so there will be no scorching. Once a full boil is reached, continue to stir and boil for five minutes. Remove from heat, stir in chocolate pieces until melted. Quickly stir in the marshmallow creme, vanilla and nuts until blended. Pour into an 8 x 8-inch pan that has been buttered. Cool, cover and keep refrigerated. Cut in squares to serve. It will keep fresh about 2 weeks but it needs to be kept refrigerated.

PEANUT BUTTER FUDGE

2 cups sugar
½ cup milk

1 square chocolate,
    shaved

Mix these 3 ingredients in a saucepan, using medium heat, bring to a boil. Boil 6 minutes, stirring and taking care this does not scorch. Remove pan from heat. Add:

1 cup peanut butter   1 cup marshmallow creme

Beat these in, then add:

1 teaspoon vanilla   ½ cup chopped nuts
Lump of butter

Beat quickly and turn into a buttered 9 x 9-inch pan.

OLD-FASHIONED CHOCOLATE FUDGE

2 cups sugar   2 tablespoons butter
2/3 cup milk   1 teaspoon vanilla
2 squares chocolate   1 cup coarsely chopped
2 tablespoons light   walnuts
  corn syrup

Put sugar, milk, chocolate that has been cut up (to make it melt easier) and corn syrup into saucepan and cook slowly, stirring until sugar is dissolved and boiling point is reached. Reduce heat and cook without stirring, but don't let it burn, until 236 degrees is reached on a candy thermometer or, when tested in cold water, it forms a soft ball. Add butter and vanilla but do not stir while cooling. When lukewarm, beat until fudge has lost its shiny look and when a small amount dropped from a spoon will hold its shape. Add walnut meats, pour into greased pan. When cold, cut into squares.

PEANUT POPCORN BALLS

Make 7 quarts salted popped corn. You could buy this all popped. Of course it isn't going to be as much fun, but sometimes it is easier.

SYRUP

2/3 cup water   1 and ¾ cups molasses
1 tablespoon vinegar   ½ teaspoon soda
½ teaspoon salt   1 cup crunchy-style
2 cups sugar   peanut butter

Mix first five ingredients in a large saucepan, bring to a boil. Using a candy thermometer, cook to 244 degrees or to hard ball stage if you do not own a thermometer. Add soda. Stir to mix.

Using a large pan or bowl, pour syrup over popped corn. Turn the peanut butter on top of syrup. Mix all together, using a wooden spoon. When completely mixed, butter hands and make into balls.

OVEN ROASTED PECANS

Place one pound shelled pecans in a 7 x 11-inch pan. Put 3 tablespoons butter and 3 tablespoons olive oil in pan. Place in a 375-degree oven. As soon as butter has melted in pan, stir to coat each nut with butter and oil. Bake, stirring occasionally, until pecans are a toasty brown in color. Since they are brown anyway, take care you do not get them too brown. You want to keep the delicate pecan flavor. About 25 to 30 minutes will be long enough.

Turn contents into a large brown paper bag. Shake well to remove excess fat. Split open the bag, salt toasted pecans lightly, and allow them to cool in opened bag.

PIES

★The usual pie crust recipes appear in most cookbooks and, strange as it seems, it is the unusual that many cooks prefer and seem to have better success in using. It is that way with oil pastry that is in Cooking Down East. Another unusual recipe is for vinegar pie crust, and over and over you will hear people remark, "I never could make decent pie crust. This recipe is the answer."

VINEGAR PIE CRUST
Enough pastry for two 2-crusted pies

FIRST PART	SECOND PART
Measure 4 cups unsifted flour into cup by spoonfuls	Beat with egg beater ½ cup cold water 1 tablespoon vinegar 1 egg
Sift together with 1 tablespoon sugar 2 teaspoons salt	Combine two mixtures. If you do not intend using all of pastry when made, store in plastic wrap in refrigerator.
Using pastry blender, cut in 1 and ¾ cups vegetable shortening	

★It is hard to believe the popularity of custard pies in Maine families. For a wife to be an accomplished custard pie maker is just about the ultimate. If she happens to make this one, she will have more fun baking it than any other recipe. It is amazing that it bakes in exactly 15 minutes. You have to make this to believe it.

VELVETY CUSTARD PIE

Make one 9-inch unbaked pastry shell (roll out dough to little less than one-eighth inch).

FILLING

4 eggs, slightly beaten	1 teaspoon vanilla
½ cup sugar	2½ cups milk, scalded
¼ teaspoon salt	Dash of nutmeg

Thoroughly mix the eggs, sugar, salt, and vanilla. Slowly stir in the hot milk. Pour at once into unbaked pie shell. To avoid spills, it is best to fill it at the oven. Dash top of filling with nutmeg. Bake in a very hot oven of 475 degrees for 5 minutes; reduce heat to 425 degrees and bake 10 minutes longer or until a table knife inserted halfway between center and edge comes out clean. Place pie on rack to cool. Serves 6 or, if custard pie is your favorite, cut it in quarters.

★Mock cherry pie is as old as the hills; it is a pie that has been baked in Maine families for generations. Cranberries, one of the chief ingredients in this filling, grow in many parts of Maine so it is no wonder that husbands recall the Mock Cherry Pie their mothers used to make, for the ingredients were right at hand.

MOCK CHERRY PIE

3 cups cranberries, chopped	1 cup water
1 cup seedless raisins, chopped	¼ teaspoon salt
	If you wish, add
1¼ cups sugar	½ teaspoon almond extract
4 tablespoons flour	2 tablespoons butter

Use pastry for a 2-crust pie.

Prepare filling by placing cranberries, raisins and water in saucepan and bring slowly to boiling point. Mix sugar, flour and salt; when cranberry mixture is boiling, add slowly to this, stirring all the time. Cook over low heat, continuing to stir until thickened. Remove from heat, add butter, stir until melted. Cool. If you wish, add almond extract.

Line 9-inch pie plate with pastry, turn mock cherry pie filling into pastry. Add top crust, flute the edges to seal. Often this pie has lattice strips of pastry for topping. Bake at 450 degrees for 10 minutes, lower heat to 350 degrees and bake about 30 minutes longer.

★This squash pie recipe has always been a mystery to me—mostly because it is in a faded old column from a newspaper. The beginning of that column could have been a sports story, but the top is torn off so I cannot tell for certain. I only know it is a wonderful recipe for squash pie. It was used by that writer's mother. She was one of six sisters, but the mystery is that I cannot tell if it is a recipe from Monroe, Maine, or if the family name was Monroe. I always felt a man wrote that column, for he stated, "Squash is a 'keeping' vegetable, for use all through the months while God is writing with the chalk of winter on the blackboard of the land."

MONROE SQUASH PIE

1½ cups cooked squash, strained, or use canned squash
¼ cup sugar
½ teaspoon salt
¼ teaspoon cinnamon
¼ teaspoon ginger

¼ teaspoon nutmeg
2 eggs, beaten lightly
1 and ¾ cups light cream, scalded
(The Monroe admonition was, "if you don't have the cream don't make the pie.")

Canned squash will be the easy way to make this pie. It is what I use. Mix squash with sugar, salt and spices. Add lightly beaten eggs. Stir in the scalded cream.

Fit pastry onto a 9-inch pie plate, flute edge. Pour prepared filling into unbaked pastry. Bake 15 minutes at 450 degrees, lower heat to 325 degrees and bake 35 minutes longer.

★Old-timers in Maine are more apt to refer to Decoration Day than to Memorial Day. It was the day set aside originally in memory of those who had died for the Union in the Civil War. It was a remembering day, just as it is today. Memorial Day has always meant a lot to me, for my Grandfather Holbrook was a Civil War veteran and once he returned home and built his farm at East Harpswell, he worked very hard for the veterans in his town. The first time I ever ate rhubarb was at my grandfather's farm. Our rhubarb season in Maine rolls around at about Memorial Day time and I never make a rhubarb pie that my thoughts do not turn to East Harpswell and the Cranberry Horn area, as it is called.

This rhubarb pie is not old-fashioned. It is very much on the Now side, for it is made with frozen strawberries as well as fresh rhubarb, and it is a delicious pie.

RHUBARB-STRAWBERRY PIE

3 cups diced, fresh rhubarb
One 10-ounce package
    frozen strawberries
3 tablespoons minute
    tapioca
¾ to 1 cup sugar

¼ teaspoon salt
1 tablespoon lemon juice
2 tablespoons melted butter
Pastry for a 2-crust pie

Defrost the frozen strawberries. Mix all ingredients together, except the melted butter. Allow these to stand for 15 minutes. In the meantime, prepare the bottom pastry for the 9-inch pie plate. Spread 1 tablespoon of the melted butter over this pastry. Fill with rhubarb-strawberry mixture. Dribble rest of melted butter over this. Cover with top pastry, flute edges. Bake at 425 degrees for 35 minutes, lower heat to 325 degrees and bake about 15 minutes longer.

Live and learn, I have found if I cut 3 small slits in the top pastry for berry or fruit pies, I have fewer boilovers. You try it.

★The baking of a pie shell sometimes presents a problem. You know, they have a way of sliding down into the pie plate as they bake. If you try to roll the pastry so it will overhang the edge of the plate about 4 inches, that helps. Place it on the plate and let it sort of relax for a few minutes. After that, using your fingers, mold it into the plate before you flute the edge of the pastry. Fold the overhanging pastry underneath as you bring it to the rim of the pie plate, flute the pastry, then gently wet your forefinger with cold water and wet the rim of the plate under the fluting, neating it up as you go around the plate. Prick unbaked pastry in several places using a table fork. Bake pie shell at 450 degrees for 15 to 18 minutes.

★That wonderful old standard, chocolate cream pie, is a favorite. This recipe came from Prospect Harbor—now that is really down east. This woman's daughter, who lives in Gardiner, says she has never found a chocolate pie as good as her mother used to make. I will vouch for that and you do, too, if you have ever sampled it at one of the card parties held for the benefit of the Gardiner General Hospital.

CHOCOLATE CREAM PIE
Recipe for an 8-inch pie:

1½ cups milk, scalded in top of double boiler	¼ teaspoon salt
2 egg yolks	1 teaspoon vanilla
1 cup sugar	1 tablespoon butter
3 tablespoons flour	2 egg whites, saved for meringue topping
3 tablespoons cocoa	

This is correct amount for an 8-inch baked pie shell. If you have a 10-inch pie in mind, double amount of this filling with the thought you will have some extra, which you can use for pudding.

Reserve 4 tablespoons of the sugar for the meringue. In making meringue, it is 2 tablespoons sugar to 1 egg white.

Mix remaining sugar, flour, cocoa and salt; beat 2 egg yolks and combine with dry mixture. Add small amount scalded milk to mixture, stir, then pour back into top of double boiler. Stir constantly over boiling water until thickened. Cover and cook about 6 minutes longer. Stir in butter.

Remove from heat, allow to cool. Add vanilla. Turn into baked pie shell. Top with meringue, bake as directed for meringue.

Many people prefer whipped topping on chocolate cream pie. If so, use all of sugar in this filling. But do not add egg whites. Reserve them for another time, for the filling would be too runny. Place in a covered jar in refrigerator.

MERINGUE FOR PIES

Use 2 tablespoons sugar for each egg white. Beat whites until they are glossy on top and when you invert the bowl, they should remain in place. Fold sugar slowly into beaten whites.

When putting meringue on pie filling, be sure you seal it carefully to the crust edge of the pie. A good way to do this is to pile meringue on center of filling, then work toward the edges. Bake meringue at 350 degrees for 15 to 20 minutes.

★French Cherry Pie comes to us from our Home Economist friend in Portland. Ever so many people have remarked to me, "You won't forget Edith's pie, will you?" You see, I did before. But not this time.

FRENCH CHERRY PIE

One baked 9-inch pie shell:

One 3-ounce package cream cheese	**1 cup cream, whipped**
½ cup confectioners' sugar	**One 1-pound, 5-ounce cherry pie filling**
½ teaspoon almond extract	

Have cream cheese at room temperature. Sift confectioners' sugar, combine with cream cheese and almond extract. Whip one cup of cream until stiff, fold thoroughly into cheese mixture. Turn into baked pie shell. Spoon cherry pie filling over top. Place pie in refrigerator and chill at least 4 hours or overnight. Serves 6.

RASPBERRY CHIFFON PIE

One baked 9-inch pie shell:

15 ounces frozen
  raspberries
    (a little less than 2
    small packages)
2 tablespoons sugar
1 tablespoon unflavored
  gelatin
¼ cup cold water

½ cup boiling water
1 tablespoon lemon juice
Pinch of salt
½ cup heavy cream,
  whipped
2 egg whites,
  beaten stiffly

Empty raspberries into a bowl, add sugar and allow to thaw. Soften gelatin in cold water, add hot water and stir until gelatin is dissolved. Crush berries with a fork. Add gelatin mixture, lemon juice and pinch of salt. Chill until slightly thickened. Whip cream, fold into raspberry mixture. Beat egg whites and fold in. Turn into baked pie shell, place in refrigerator and chill until firm.

★Mile high strawberry pie is exactly that! It is also delicious, beautiful and an unbelievable pie. This pie requires a baked pie shell. After the filling is turned into the shell, the pie is frozen.

MILE HIGH STRAWBERRY PIE

One baked 9-inch pie shell:

One 10-ounce package
  frozen strawberries
2 egg whites
Pinch of salt

¾ cup granulated sugar
1 tablespoon lemon juice
½ cup heavy cream,
  whipped
1 teaspoon vanilla

Make certain the larger bowl of your electric mixer and the beaters are spotlessly clean, for otherwise egg whites may not beat up as they should.

Place bowl and beaters in refrigerator to chill. Thaw strawberries to a mushy state. Make certain this is a 10-ounce package of frozen strawberries. If you use a pound package, it will be a dismal failure.

Turn mushy strawberries into chilled bowl with the unbeaten egg whites, salt, sugar and lemon juice. Beat this mixture at highest speed on your electric mixer for 15 minutes. In meantime, beat the ½ cup heavy cream in a smaller bowl using a regular beater. Add vanilla to this. Gently fold into the strawberry mixture. At this point the larger bowl of your mixer will be completely filled. Turn into baked pie shell. Swirl top. Place pie uncovered in freezer. It is served frozen. Serves 6 generously; it will serve 8 amply. Three to four days is about as long as you will want to keep this pie in your freezer.

★This is not a State-of-Maine-ish pie at all, but chances are you have made it because it is such a good pie—especially for parties. If you have adopted it as a favorite, then it should not be left out of this cookbook.

MANDARIN ORANGE PIE

One baked 9-inch pie shell:

One package, 3 and ¾ ounce instant pudding mix, banana or pineapple cream
One package, 4¼ ounce whipped topping mix— use both envelopes
2 cups milk

½ teaspoon vanilla
2 bananas
1 pound can mandarin oranges, drained
Flaked cocoanut

Slice bananas and line bottom of baked pie shell. Arrange drained mandarin oranges on top of bananas, reserving several for top decoration.

Beat together in a bowl the dry pudding mix, dry topping mix, 2 cups milk and vanilla. Beat only until it begins to thicken. Pour over oranges and place pie in refrigerator. Allow pie to stay in refrigerator 15 minutes, giving the filling a chance to become thick.

Remove pie and decorate top center with remaining orange sections. Sprinkle flaked cocoanut around them. Place pie back in refrigerator for 2 hours to chill before serving. Serves 6 to 8.

★Maine is a great egg-producing state and recipes like angel pie have great appeal. Most pies of this kind say to refrigerate; this does not. Easy to make and quick, too.

ANGEL PIE

6 egg whites	1 tablespoon vinegar
2 cups sugar	¼ teaspoon salt
1 teaspoon vanilla	1 cup cream, whipped for topping

Butter and flour a 9-inch pie plate. Beat the 6 egg whites but not too stiff. Add 1 cup of the sugar gradually. Continue beating and add salt. Add the second cup of sugar gradually but alternately with the one tablespoon vinegar. Add vanilla.

Turn into prepared pie plate. Bring meringue to edge but mound it up in the center.

Bake one hour in all—at 275 degrees for 30 minutes, then at 300 degrees for 30 minutes. This pie should never be refrigerated.

Place pie on rack and when cool spread it with 1 cup cream, whipped. Serve each piece topped with frozen raspberries, strawberries or peaches. Serves 6.

★Oatmeal pie is Maine's answer to pecan pie. Since it tastes almost identical, contains no nuts and uses ingredients you would be certain to have on hand, it is very popular.

OATMEAL PIE

¾ cup quick oatmeal, uncooked	1 stick margarine, melted
¾ cup dark corn syrup	¾ cup milk
1 cup sugar	2 eggs, beaten
1 cup flaked cocoanut	Pinch of salt
	½ teaspoon vanilla

Combine all ingredients, pour into a 9-inch unbaked pie crust. Bake at 350 degrees for 40 minutes. Place pie on rack to cool. If you wish, serve with a dollop of whipped cream.

★I've had more fun with this recipe than any other that ever appeared in my column. It's pure fun all the way. This is the pie you serve to your family on April Fool's Day and never say one word. Before it ever appeared in my column, I had it in my file for two years; didn't even try it. My mother and father had dear friends in West Bath and it was Lizzie who sent the recipe to me. Someone in Bath brought it back from a convention, but that's the way recipes travel. Finally, I made the pie and I like thinking that Lizzie and I promoted this recipe. After all, that was a long time ago. It was when a friend of ours who was a judge said, "This tastes the most like the apple pie my mother used to make," that made me laugh the most. I never told him the difference.

MYSTERY PIE

12 saltines, single ones	1 teaspoon nutmeg
1 ½ cups sugar	1 teaspoon cinnamon
1 ½ cups cold water	Bits of butter
1 ½ teaspoons cream of tartar	Pastry, for a 2-crust pie

Break up saltines into a bowl, as you would for "crackers and milk." Add sugar, cream of tartar, nutmeg and cinnamon. Stir in cold water, using a table fork. No salt in this recipe; there is enough on the crackers. Allow mixture to set while rolling out pie crust for a 9-inch pie plate.

Place lower crust on pie plate. Roll out top pie crust before you pour filling into pie plate. All ready? Pour filling into plate, dot with bits of butter or margarine all over this sloppy mess. Place top crust on pie, then cut 3 small slits in top center of crust to allow steam to escape. Flute edges of pastry.

Bake at 425 degrees for 40 minutes. You will have a pie that tastes exactly like apple pie. And don't tell your family.

PUDDINGS

★If ever a recipe has stood the test of time, it has to be Judge Peters Pudding. In 1883 John A. Peters of Bangor was appointed Chief Justice of the Maine Supreme Court. This was his favorite dessert, which he enjoyed especially at holiday time. It is not at all the sort of recipe you might expect at the turn of the century, and we like to think he will be remembered among other things for this fine dessert.

JUDGE PETERS PUDDING

Soak 2 envelopes plain
  gelatin in ½ cup cold
  water, each envelope is
  1 tablespoon
Add 1 cup boiling water
½ cup fresh orange juice
1 cup sugar
Stir to dissolve ingredients
  and chill until syrupy

Combine in a bowl
2 oranges, cut in pieces
2 bananas, sliced
6 figs, cut small
9 dates, cut small
10 walnuts,
  broken coarsely
Juice of 2 lemons

When the gelatin mixture begins to congeal, fold in the fruit mixture, blend well. Pour into a mold and chill until set. Custard cups make good molds for individual servings. Top with whipped cream or a custard sauce, although it is delicious just as it is.

When preparing fruits, use kitchen shears dipped in hot water. It makes the job go faster.

OLD FASHIONED BREAD PUDDING

1 quart milk, scalded
2 cups soft bread crumbs,
  packed lightly
2 eggs
1/3 cup sugar

½ teaspoon salt
1 teaspoon vanilla
¼ teaspoon nutmeg
¼ cup melted butter or
  margarine

Add bread crumbs to scalded milk. Beat eggs slightly, add sugar and salt, mix thoroughly. Gradually stir in the milk and bread crumbs, vanilla, nutmeg and butter. Pour into buttered 1½-quart casserole, set in pan of warm water. Bake at 350 degrees for 75 minutes or until a table knife inserted in center comes out clean. Serves 6 to 8.

Try squeezing fresh lemon juice on top of warm pudding when it is removed from oven. Cool to lukewarm, serve with whipped or plain cream.

★This recipe for cinnamon apples is remembered from that long ago fall day when the Burton Crosses entertained at the Blaine House for the food editors from the eastern part of the nation, who were touring Maine. This dessert showed off Maine apples better than any other way.

BAKED CINNAMON APPLES

6 large tart baking apples	½ cup sugar, to use
½ cup seedless raisins	in glaze
¼ cup chopped nuts	¾ cup water
2 tablespoons sugar,	Pinch of salt
to mix with fruit	Grated rind of 1 lemon
1 teaspoon cornstarch	4 teaspoons lemon juice
	1 tablespoon red
	cinnamon candies

Wash and core apples, pare a third of way down from stem end. Place in 1½-quart baking dish, with pared side up. Combine raisins, nuts and the 2 tablespoons sugar. Fill center of each apple with mixture.

Combine cornstarch and ½ cup sugar in saucepan. This is for the glaze. Add lemon rind, juice, water, salt and cinnamon candies. Cook over a medium heat until syrup boils and candies melt.

Pour hot sauce over apples in baking dish and bake at 350 degrees about 60 minutes or until apples are tender. Baste often, so apples will be glazed. Even after pan is placed on rack for cooling, continue to do this. Serve with a custard sauce or whipped topping. Or plain.

If you prefer a more simple procedure for baking apples, then wash, wipe and core your favorite McIntosh,

Northern Spy or Cortland apples. Pare one strip around center of apples or down about a quarter of the way. Place prepared fruit in baking dish. Mix ½ cup sugar with ½ teaspoon cinnamon for 6 apples. Spoon this into cavities of apples. Cover bottom of dish with boiling water, bake at 400 degrees until soft, basting with syrup in dish. Serve hot or cold with cream.

BAKED APPLE PUDDING

2 cups diced or thinly   Juice of ½ lemon
  sliced apples   ½ teaspoon cinnamon

Butter an 8 x 8-inch pan, turn apples into pan, dribble lemon juice over them and sprinkle cinnamon over apples.

¾ cup sugar   1 teaspoon baking powder
3 tablespoons margarine   ¼ teaspoon salt
1 cup sifted flour   ½ cup milk

Cream margarine and sugar and add sifted dry ingredients alternately with milk. There are no eggs in the recipe. Spread the batter all over the top of the apples.

1 cup sugar   Dash of salt
1 tablespoon cornstarch   1 cup boiling water

Mix sugar, salt and cornstarch. Turn this dry mixture all over the batter. Then pour the 1 cup boiling water over the top.

Bake at 375 degrees 1 hour. Serve warm, topped with a small serving of vanilla ice cream or a whipped cream topping. It is also especially nice served plain. Serves 8.

EASIEST DESSERT

Heat in top of double boiler over boiling water:
2/3 cup milk   Pinch of salt
¼ cup sugar   1 teaspoon vanilla
1 square chocolate

Allow these ingredients to heat, then beat until smooth. Drop in 2 unbeaten eggs, begin immediately to beat, and do a good job at it. If you use a hand beater, beat one full minute; with an electric beater about ½ minute will do the trick. Cover top of double boiler and cook over boiling water for 30 minutes. Spoon into serving dishes. Serve hot or cold with plain or whipped cream. Serves 4.

STOVE-TOP
PEANUT BUTTER CUSTARD

3 eggs	1 tall can
1/3 cup sugar	evaporated milk
¼ teaspoon salt	½ tablespoon vanilla
1/3 cup peanut butter	1 cup boiling water

Beat first 3 ingredients. Put peanut butter in a bowl and stir in the evaporated milk, vanilla and then the boiling water. Stir this into the egg mixture and ladle into 6 to 8 greased custard cups. Place cups on a rack in large skillet or two small skillets. Pour hot water into the skillet until it comes up to the depth of the mixture in the custard cups. Bring this water to a full boil. Cover skillet, remove pan from heat and let stand for 20 minutes or until custard is set.

Remove custard cups from water, cool, place in refrigerator to chill. Unmold and serve plain or, if you wish, with:

CHOCOLATE SAUCE

One 6-ounce package semi-   ¾ cup evaporated milk
sweet chocolate bits

Stir these two ingredients together in saucepan, using a medium heat. When chocolate is melted and ingredients are well blended, remove from heat. Cool.

★The carpets of blue you see from the roadside as you ride around Maine during the month of August are ripe, low-bush Maine blueberries. They are nature's convenience food, for there is nothing to do to them except wash them and enjoy them just as they are. For generations Maine families have been picking these delicious wild blueberries, and you can plan on most families having a secret spot where they do this picking. Maybe it is not your good fortune to be able to pick your own but you can whiff the box of freshly picked blueberries you have bought and almost get a smell of pine.

If the fields you see are carpeted with Maine blueberries, then you know they are being produced commercially. Crews harvest the berries by hand with small blueberry rakes. Most of the crop is frozen or canned at processing plants and distributed throughout the country. Some blueberries are sold fresh. In any form Maine blueberries are delicious.

A chilled jar of blueberry sauce is good to have in your refrigerator. A heavenly (blue, of course) dessert is blueberry sauce on lemon sherbet. Try blueberry sauce on French toast, pancakes or waffles.

BLUEBERRY SAUCE

½ cup sugar
2 teaspoons cornstarch
Dash of salt
½ cup water

1 pint blueberries
1 tablespoon lemon juice
1 teaspoon grated
   lemon rind

Combine sugar, cornstarch and salt. Stir in the water. Add blueberries and bring to boil. Simmer until clear and thickened, about 4 minutes, continuing to stir. Remove from heat, add lemon juice and rind. Sometimes folding in an extra cup of uncooked blueberries adds a special flavor, but is not necessary.

★This recipe stirs memories. The summer I cooked at Camp Brookline, a girls' camp in Bridgton, this was their favorite dessert. It could have been because the girls picked their own blueberries. We called it blueberry bread and butter pudding; come to find out, it is named Blueberry Flummery. Actually the recipe is as old as New England. It is simple to make and delicious.

BLUEBERRY FLUMMERY

8 slices bread, buttered
1 quart blueberries
1 cup sugar

1 teaspoon salt
Whipped topping

Wash the berries, place in saucepan, add sugar and salt, cook over low heat to simmering point. Cook for 10 minutes.

Butter bread generously. Trim crusts. Alternate layers of buttered bread and hot stewed blueberries until all are used, ending with fruit and juice. Bake at 350 degrees for 20 minutes. Chill in refrigerator. Top with whipped cream flavored with nutmeg.

BLUEBERRY SLUMP

2 cups blueberries, washed   2 teaspoons baking powder
½ cup sugar   ¼ teaspoon salt
1 cup water   About ½ cup milk
1 cup sifted flour

Stew blueberries, sugar and water in saucepan. Mix and sift flour, baking powder and salt, add milk, stirring quickly to make a dumpling dough that will drop from the end of a spoon. Drop into the boiling sauce. The dumplings should measure from 1½ to 2 inches. Cover pan tightly and cook about 15 to 20 minutes. Spoon the dumplings into shallow soup plates, covering them with the blueberry sauce. Serve with slightly sweetened whipped cream or plain cream. This is also called Blueberry Grunt.

JIFFY RHUBARB DESSERT

4 cups rhubarb, cut up   2 cups yellow or white
1 cup sugar   cake mix, used dry
One 3-ounce package   1 cup cold water
    strawberry gelatin,   5 tablespoons melted
    used dry   margarine

Butter an oblong pan, about 7 x 10 inches. Place the raw, cut-up rhubarb in pan, sprinkle with sugar, then strawberry gelatin, used dry. Sprinkle the 2 cups dry cake mix all over gelatin. Gently pour the cup of water over all and dribble the melted margarine over the top. Bake 1 hour at 350 degrees. Serve warm or cold with your favorite topping. Serves 8.

★Just because I cannot bear the name of this delicious dessert, I am going to change the title. This recipe has been a wonderful idea for club meetings and we are very grateful to the Augusta friend who shared it. Oh well, the name was Dump Cake.

EASY DESSERT FOR 12

One 16-ounce can
  crushed pineapple
One can pie filling (your
  choice) (Mine's cherry)

One regular-size package
  yellow or white cake mix
1½ sticks margarine

Butter a 9 x 13-inch pan. Turn undrained crushed pineapple into pan and spread around pan. Cover with pie filling. Spread dry cake mix all over fruit. Slice 1½ sticks margarine all over cake mix. Bake 1 hour at 350 degrees. May be served lukewarm or cold. Cut in squares. Top with ice cream or whipped topping. Serves 12.

GLORIFIED RICE

½ cup raw rice
2 cups milk
¼ teaspoon salt
½ cup sugar

2 tablespoons plain gelatin
1 cup cream, to whip
1 teaspoon vanilla

Cook rice your favorite way. When cooked, combine with milk, salt and sugar in top of double boiler. When well-heated, combine with the 2 tablespoons plain gelatin that has been soaked in one scant cup cold water. Mix well. Turn into bowl and place in refrigerator until mixture is nearly "set." This makes a fluffier dessert. Whip one cup cream. Fold into rice and gelatin mixture. Add vanilla. Turn into 7 x 11-inch pan. Place in refrigerator until firm. Cut in squares. Serve with:

HOT BUTTERSCOTCH SAUCE

½ cup granulated sugar
½ cup brown sugar
½ cup light cream

¼ teaspoon salt
1 teaspoon vanilla
Small piece of butter

Mix sugars, cream and salt. Cook in saucepan over a medium heat for 15 minutes. Remove from heat. Add vanilla and butter. Serve hot.

GAR'S WONDERFUL DESSERT

1 cup milk	1 tablespoon gelatin
1 egg, beaten	½ cup cold water
3 tablespoons sugar	1 cup cream

Heat milk in top of double boiler. In meantime, beat egg and sugar together. Pour a little of the hot milk into egg, stir, then pour back into top of double boiler. Cook together, stirring constantly until mixture coats a silver spoon. Remove from heat.

Allow gelatin to dissolve in cold water, add to custard mixture, stir well. Place mixture in refrigerator until it begins to thicken. Whip 1 cup cream and fold into the thickened mixture. Pour into serving dish and chill until set. This dessert may be made a day or so in advance. Spoon into serving dishes and top with the following sauce:

CHOCOLATE SAUCE

One 6-ounce package semi-sweet chocolate bits	¼ teaspoon salt
	1 cup hot water
½ cup sugar	1 teaspoon vanilla

Measure all ingredients into saucepan. Bring to a boil, stirring constantly and cook slowly for 3 minutes. Cool, add one teaspoon vanilla. Chill. Serve chilled on top of chilled pudding.

CORNFLAKE PUDDING

2 heaping cups cornflakes	1 egg
2 cups milk	½ teaspoon salt
½ cup molasses	½ cup seedless raisins or cut-up dates

This pudding is cooked in the top of a double boiler, so it may be mixed in it also. Place the egg in top part, beat egg slightly, add milk, beat with egg beater to mix well. Add salt and molasses. Stir in cornflakes and raisins. Place cover on top of double boiler, place over boiling water; keep this water in lower part of double boiler at a slow boil. Cook one hour. Serve warm or cold topped with vanilla ice cream or plain cream. Serves 4.

★It was springtime when this delicious sherbet recipe was given to me. After hearing about it, I asked, "May I call it Spring Fling Sherbet?" For all people on a low-fat diet, it was a blessing.

SPRING FLING SHERBET

One 16-ounce can evaporated skimmed milk
1 cup granulated sugar

One 6-ounce can frozen fruit juice of your choice. Use frozen lemonade if that is your favorite.

Evaporated skimmed milk contains less than one per cent butter fat. Once it is chilled you will be able to whip it.

Place can of milk in refrigerator for several hours or overnight. Allow the frozen fruit juice to thaw but keep it chilled. Also chill the bowl and beaters so the milk will whip up quickly.

Open can of milk and whip until it holds up in peaks. This takes just a few minutes. Slowly add sugar. Open small can frozen juice that has been thawed, add slowly. That's it! Ladle into plastic containers. Cover containers and place in freezer. This makes 2½ quarts of sherbet. Allow to freeze. No beating, no stirring. This smooth, delicious dessert will keep for 3 or 4 weeks in your freezer.

QUICK LEMON FRUIT BOWL

One 17-ounce can fruit cocktail
One 11-ounce can Mandarin oranges
One small can pineapple chunks

One 3-ounce package instant lemon pudding mix
1 tablespoon lemon juice
½ cup flaked cocoanut
1 banana, sliced

Mix undrained fruit, lemon juice, cocoanut, then add dry instant pudding mix. Stir gently and place in refrigerator to chill. Just before serving add sliced banana. Serve in sauce dishes — if you happen to have a glass bowl it is nice to serve this fruit dessert at the table.

PRETZEL DESSERT

Using an 11 x 13-inch pan, press following crust into it. You do not need to butter the pan, since a half pound melted butter or margarine is used in the crust.

2 cups pretzels, crushed no smaller than ¼ inch
3 tablespoons sugar

½ pound butter or margarine, melted and stirred into crumbs and sugar

FILLING

One 8-ounce package cream cheese
1/3 cup lemon juice

1 can condensed milk (sweetened)
1 teaspoon vanilla

Beat together, using a mixer. Turn all over crust in pan. Top with canned strawberry-rhubarb pie filling or canned cherry pie filling. Place in refrigerator. Do not freeze. Serves 12 to 15.

JEWEL TARTS

CRUST

¾ cup graham cracker crumbs

Combine with
½ stick butter or margarine, melted

This recipe makes 16 tarts. Using regular size paper crinkle cups, place two, one inside the other, in regular-size muffin tins. Divide crumb mixture evenly in the 16 cups. Using a glass, press the mixture down in crinkle cups. Bake crust at 375 degrees for 10 minutes.

FILLING

One 8-ounce package cream cheese
1 egg

½ cup granulated sugar
½ teaspoon vanilla

Beat egg until thick, add sugar and vanilla, combine with softened cream cheese. Spoon into paper cups, onto cooled baked crust. Divide evenly. Top with canned pie filling of your choice, spooning it onto each tart. Choose all one kind or vary topping like cherry, pineapple, or blueberry. It is more expensive to vary them but this is the reason they are called jewel tarts.

STRAWBERRY DESSERT

1 large angel cake,
  broken into not too small
  bite-size pieces
One 6-ounce package
  strawberry gelatin
2 cups boiling water

1-pound package
  frozen strawberries
1 pint cream, whipped, or
  2 envelopes dessert topping, whipped according
  to directions

Use one large store-bought angel cake. Break into pieces, not too tiny. Place in a large bowl. In another bowl put contents of large package of strawberry gelatin. Pour in boiling water, stir to dissolve. Place the block of frozen strawberries in hot mixture. As the strawberries melt, the mixture thickens. Whip the cream, then lightly combine the angel cake pieces, the thickened strawberry gelatin mixture, and the whipped cream. Turn carefully into a lightly-oiled large angel cake pan or into oiled 9 x 13-inch pan, which may be served more easily in squares. Place dessert in refrigerator. Chill several hours or overnight. Serves 16.

★It was bound to happen, for someone made a similar dessert using the angel cake, the whipped cream and a chocolate mixture. And you guessed it, the name is Golf Ball Dessert. It is a popular dessert, and you may be certain the name has something to do with it.

GOLF BALL DESSERT

One 12-ounce package
  semi-sweet chocolate bits
2 tablespoons water
2 tablespoons sugar
4 egg yolks, slightly beaten
1 tablespoon plain gelatin

2 tablespoons cold water
4 egg whites, beaten stiff
1 pint cream, whipped
One large angel cake,
  broken into golf ball
  size pieces

Combine chocolate bits, water, sugar and slightly beaten egg yolks in top of double boiler. Cook over slowly boiling water until chocolate bits are melted and mixture is thickened. Mix plain gelatin with 2 tablespoons cold water to dissolve it. Just before removing chocolate mixture from heat, stir into top of double boiler, continuing to stir so gelatin is completely melted. Remove from heat. Cool this mixture.

Beat egg whites until stiff. Whip cream until stiff. Break large angel cake into golf-ball-size pieces. Fold these three ingredients together, then fold in cooled chocolate mixture. Oil lightly a 9 x 13-inch pan, turn dessert mixture into this. Place in refrigerator to chill for 24 hours. Cut in squares to serve. Serves 16 to 20.

LIME DELIGHT

One tall can evaporated milk (14½ ounce)
One 3-ounce package lime gelatin
1 and ¾ cups boiling water
1 cup sugar
¼ cup lime juice
2 teaspoons lemon juice
2 cups chocolate cookie crumbs
½ cup melted butter or margarine
Shaved semi-sweet or bitter chocolate for topping

Chill can of evaporated milk until very cold, like overnight in the refrigerator. Dissolve gelatin in boiling water. Chill until partially set. Combine chocolate crumbs with melted butter and press into 11½ x 7½-inch pan.

Whip lime gelatin until fluffy. Stir in sugar and fruit juices. Whip evaporated milk until it holds up in peaks. Fold into the gelatin mixture. Turn into the crumb-lined pan. Sprinkle shaved chocolate all over top. Chill until firm. Serves 12.

FORGOTTEN DESSERT

6 egg whites
¼ teaspoon salt
½ teaspoon cream of tartar
1½ cups sugar
1 teaspoon vanilla

Preheat oven to 450 degrees.

Beat egg whites and salt together until they are frothy. Add the ½ teaspoon cream of tartar and continue beating whites until they are stiff. Add the 1½ cups sugar, a teaspoon at a time. Add vanilla and continue beating about 10 minutes longer.

Use a buttered 9 x 9-inch pan. Turn mixture into pan. Place pan in oven, immediately turn off the heat. Leave dessert in oven all day or all night for you are baking this dessert on stored heat. Do you see why it is called forgotten dessert?

After all day or all night, remove pan from oven, spread top of dessert with ½ cup cream, whipped. Add 2 tablespoons confectioners' sugar to this and spread all over top of dessert. Set pan in refrigerator to chill.

Serve in squares. Top each square with crushed berries or frozen fruit. Serves 9.

★Sharing sauce it is called nowadays. There is nothing new about this delicious fruit sauce, for many a butt'ry or cellar boasted a crock of this sauce ready for ladling generously onto a plate of vanilla ice cream or a slice of pound or sponge cake. A few years ago a cup of this sauce and the recipe were shared by our friend Betty, who lives in Portland. As soon as I used the recipe in my column I received interesting letters. One woman in Unity wrote, "When I was a little girl I used to dip into this sauce occasionally when an errand took me down cellar." This sauce has enjoyed a great revival, and now most Maine kitchens have a glass crock of sharing sauce on their counters.

SHARING SAUCE

The idea is that someone will share one cup of her sauce with you and that will start you on your own way. You will add fruit and sugar to this and soon you will be using and sharing your own sauce. If you have been so favored by a friend, then every two weeks you will proceed as follows:

Add 1 small can peaches, drained and cut up	**5 maraschino cherries, cut up**
2 slices pineapple, cut up	**1 cup sugar**

Let stand 10 minutes, then stir. Stir every three days. Keep in a covered jar. Do not refrigerate. Ladle onto a serving of vanilla ice cream or a slice of sponge cake. When sharing, give a cup but always keep a cup for yourself.

What if your friend does not have a crock of sharing sauce? You will make your own "starter," using one package of dry yeast.

STARTER FOR FRUIT SAUCE

¾ cup drained canned
  peaches, cut in pieces
¾ cup drained
  pineapple bits

6 maraschino cherries,
  cut in half
1½ cups sugar
1 package dry yeast

Combine ingredients and place in a glass jar with a loose cover — an apothecary jar is perfect. Stir several times the first day, then stir once a day. At the end of two weeks the starter has fermented enough to make sauce. Makes 2 cups.

★These next desserts may be made any time of year, but in Maine we like to think they are holiday desserts.

SNOW PUDDING

1 tablespoon plain gelatin
¼ cup cold water
1 cup boiling water
¾ cup sugar
Pinch of salt

1 tablespoon grated
  lemon rind
¼ cup lemon juice
2 or 3 egg whites

Soak gelatin in cold water 5 minutes, add boiling water and stir until gelatin is dissolved. Add ½ cup of the sugar, salt, lemon rind and juice. Stir to dissolve and chill until thickened. Beat egg whites until quite stiff, add remaining sugar and beat until stiff. Beat into thickened pudding, using an egg beater. Turn into a quart mold that has been rinsed with cold water. Chill until set, unmold and serve with custard sauce.

CUSTARD SAUCE

2 tablespoons sugar
Pinch of salt
2 or 3 egg yolks left
from pudding

2 teaspoons flour
1 cup milk
½ teaspoon vanilla

Mix sugar, salt, flour and beaten egg yolks in top part of double boiler; beat together, using a fork. Slowly add milk and continue beating. Have water boiling in lower part of double boiler, place top part over this and stir until sauce thickens, about 7 minutes. Remove from heat, add vanilla. Chill and serve over snow pudding.

HUNTER'S PUDDING

1 cup finely chopped suet
1 cup molasses
1 cup milk
3 cups sifted flour
1 teaspoon soda
1 teaspoon salt

½ teapsoon allspice
½ teaspoon powdered
cloves
½ teaspoon mace
1 teaspoon cinnamon
1½ cups seedless raisins
2 tablespoons flour

Sift dry ingredients together. Add molasses and milk to finely chopped suet. Combine mixtures. Coat seedless raisins with 2 tablespoons flour and add to mixture. Turn into greased mold, cover and steam for 3 hours. Grease inside of cover to prevent sticking.

If you do not have a proper mold for steaming, No. 2 tin cans (like corn comes in) or No. 2½ cans (tomatoes), well greased, will do. Cover cans with foil, taking care to fill only two-thirds full. Place cans on a rack with two or three inches of water in a large kettle, cover and cook on top of stove.

Serve this suet pudding with hard sauce or a foamy sauce, sometimes referred to as soft sauce.

HARLEQUIN HARD SAUCE

2/3 cup butter or
margarine
2 cups confectioners' sugar

Pinch of salt
½ teaspoon vanilla

Cream butter or margarine, add sugar gradually. Add salt and vanilla. Add a bit of cream if you wish. Divide into 3 parts. Color each portion to suit your fancy. For Thanksgiving use pale orange, yellow and green. For Christmas, the traditional red and green. Arrange in layers. Chill or freeze. Slice, to serve on hunter's pudding.

A CHRISTMAS PUDDING

20 graham crackers
1 cup dates, cut in very
    small pieces
14 large marshmallows,
    cut in small pieces

1 cup chopped nuts
½ cup medium cream or
    evaporated milk
Candied cherries

Roll graham crackers. The easiest way to do this is to place them in a plastic bag for rolling. Reserve about ½ cup of the crumbs. Put remainder in bowl. Cut dates and marshmallows, using kitchen shears. Add to crumbs. Add nuts and cream or evaporated milk. Stir, then mold into a roll, adding more cream if mixture seems too dry. Roll in cracker crumbs that have been reserved. Use candied cherries cut into bits and make the word YULE on one side of the roll. Wrap in foil or plastic wrap and store in refrigerator.

To serve, place on a cutting board at the table, cut in slices and top with custard sauce or a whipped topping. Serves 8.

PEPPERMINT STICK
CREAM DESSERT

12 vanilla wafers
1 pint cream, whipped
1 cup crushed peppermint
    stick candy

1 cup chopped nuts
12 large marshmallows,
    cut up
1 teaspoon vanilla
¼ teaspoon salt

Use a loaf pan, since this dessert is served sliced. Crush boughten vanilla wafers between fingers. Put part of crumbs in buttered pan, reserving some for topping. Chop nuts, saving some to mix with crumbs for topping. Place candy between 2 sheets of waxed paper, place on a board and tap gently with a hammer until fine. Measure one cupful. Using kitchen shears, cut marshmallows. Whip cream until it holds up but is not stiff.

Fold marshmallows, candy, nuts, vanilla and salt into whipped cream. Turn mixture onto crumbs in loaf pan. Sprinkle remainder of crumbs and nuts on top.

Refrigerate at least 24 hours. It may be frozen but that is not necessary. Serves 8 generously.

PINK ARCTIC FREEZE

Two 3-ounce packages
  cream cheese
2 tablespoons sugar
2 tablespoons mayonnaise
One 1-pound can whole
  cranberry sauce (2 cups)

One 9-ounce can (1 cup)
  crushed pineapple,
  drained
½ cup chopped nuts
1 cup cream, whipped

Soften cream cheese, blend in the mayonnaise and sugar. Add cranberry sauce, pineapple and nuts. Fold in the whipped cream. Turn into a loaf pan. Cover. Freeze firm. When time to serve, make certain it has been at room temperature for 15 minutes. Slice or cut in squares to serve. Makes 8 to 10 servings.

ANGEL CAKE DELIGHT

One large angel food cake
One 16-ounce can crushed
  pineapple

1 cup miniature
  marshmallows
One 9-ounce container
  whipped topping or
  1 pint cream

Break angel food cake into tiny pieces. Drain can of crushed pineapple carefully. If you decide to use cream, then it is whipped. Mix angel food pieces, drained crushed pineapple, marshmallows and whipped topping or whipped cream by folding carefully together.

This mixture may be turned into a buttered 7 x 11-inch glass pan or left in bowl in which it is mixed. Chill all day or overnight. If in a pan, it may be cut in squares and placed on individual plates for serving, topped with a maraschino cherry. If you left it in the bowl, then spoon lightly into sherbet glasses and top with a cherry. This recipe serves 8 to 10 people.

For future use...

September blow soft till the fruit's in the loft

CHAPTER TEN

For Future Use

Food preservation goes on just about year 'round in Maine. Freezing makes it ever so much easier, yet a tremendous amount of home canning is done in the Pine Tree State. Have you ever noticed the displays of canning equipment in the markets, come summer?

Men play an important part in preserving food for future use, too. From wintertime, when Maine shrimp are available for home freezers, right on through the fishing season, the canning of dandelion greens and the freezing of fiddleheads, they are helpful to their wives.

There isn't a season in Maine that doesn't provide us with food that needs preservation by some method. Most Maine families have a favorite way and menfolks like to be a part of the activity, especially when it gets to be pickling time.

We pickle early and we pickle late in Maine. Of course pickles are almost without nutritive value, but who can think of a plate of baked beans and not say, "Please pass the pickles." Sometimes you would think pickles were made for swapping. Once a batch has been made, the "swaps" are on. It's a matter of sharing.

If there is a hunter in the family, then men really come into their own when the fall season arrives. After all, a freezer with a supply of Maine's game birds and venison is good evidence there is a successful hunter in the family.

★Apple butter is a conserve, easy to make, old-fashioned and popular. It is delicious with toast and is often used as a filling for turnovers.

APPLE BUTTER

Wash apples and cut into eighths. Cut out stem end and blossom end. Place in covered saucepan, add enough cold water so it comes up in pan about one inch. Cover and cook until apples are tender. Put through a sieve or food mill. To each cup of pulp add ½ cup sugar and cook mixture in a saucepan until it is thick and clear. If the apples lack flavor, a small amount of lemon juice and grated rind or spices may be added to suit the taste.

Fill sterilized jelly jars, top with melted paraffin, cover jars and store — for future use.

SLICED STRAWBERRY JAM

4½ cups or 2 pounds prepared strawberries
7 cups or 3 pounds sugar

½ of an 8-ounce bottle liquid pectin

The strawberries are weighed and measured after they are prepared. To prepare fruit, cut about 2 quarts of fully ripe berries in halves lengthwise, large berries in quarters.

Weigh the fruit or measure it. Then measure the fruit and sugar into a large saucepan.

Mix well together and bring to a full rolling boil on a high heat. The sugar and berries need to be stirred constantly before they reach the boiling point and while they are boiling. A wooden spoon is excellent for this.

Once the boiling point is reached, boil hard for 3 minutes. Remove the kettle from heat and stir in the ½ bottle of liquid pectin. Stir and skim by turns for 5 minutes. Allow mixture to cool slightly to prevent floating fruit. Pour quickly into sterilized jelly jars. Cover at once with a thin layer of melted paraffin. Cool, then cover each jar. This recipe makes ten 6-ounce jars of jam.

ORANGE MARMALADE

1 orange
1 grapefruit

1 lemon
Granulated sugar

This is the recipe we were taught to make in foods classes when I was at Farmington. You couldn't find a better recipe, nor an easier one.

Choose clear, unblemished fruit. Wash and cut into large pieces. Remove seeds. Put fruit and skin through the food grinder.

Measure pulp by cupfuls into a large kettle. Measure and add three times as much water as fruit. Allow this to set overnight or for 24 hours.

Place kettle on stove, bring slowly to a boil and allow to boil for 15 minutes. Remove from heat and let set another 24 hours. Measure mixture and add an equal amount of sugar. Bring slowly to boiling point and cook slowly, being careful that it does not burn. This will take 2 to 2½ hours for it to become thickened to the proper marmalade consistency. To test for this, drop a little onto a saucer. If it looks as if it were about to jell, it has cooked long enough.

Turn into hot, clean glasses. Top with melted paraffin. I use this same recipe for kumquat marmalade — to 1 quart kumquats, which you will cut in half to remove seeds before grinding, add ½ lemon. It is delicious and easy to make.

CRABAPPLE JELLY

Chances are someone will offer you some crabapples, and at a time like this it is good to have a recipe for making that popular old-fashioned jelly. It will be easier if you have some scales but if you haven't, don't let that stop you from making this jelly.

Wash crabapples, remove stems and quarter apples. Put into large kettle, cover quartered apples with cold water, making certain water comes to an inch above apples. Bring to a boil, then cook over a medium heat until fruit is a mush.

In the meantime, weigh the kettle in which you will be cooking the syrup. When apples are at a mushy stage, pour the hot fruit at once into a jelly bag and hang over the kettle you have weighed. Allow this to drip until it stops, usually overnight. Do not squeeze bag or you will have a cloudy jelly.

If you do not have a jelly bag, you could line a large colander with a piece of unbleached muslin, then set this on top of the kettle. It will work but you will not get as much juice.

Place kettle and juice back on scales. Add an equal amount of sugar for amount of juice you have in kettle. Some cooks measure this strained juice by cupfuls, adding one cup sugar to each cup of juice.

Using your candy thermometer, bring this juice and sugar to a boil and cook to 222 degrees. Use a wooden spoon to stir juice and sugar, as this will not sink into the liquid. Another test for the jelly stage is to use a spoon, dipping it into the jelly and letting the syrup run off the side of the spoon. When the syrup no longer runs off the side in a steady stream but separates into two distinct lines of drops which "sheet" together, stop the cooking.

Skim the top of jelly, removing the foam, then pour immediately into sterilized glasses. Cover with a thin layer of melted paraffin. Allow jelly to cool completely before putting covers on jars.

Never melt paraffin over direct heat. Put a small pitcher of shaved or cut-up paraffin in a pan of hot water on heat and melt in this way.

★Just the other day I remarked to my Auburn friend with whom I worked many years in the power company, "Helen, I feel you are looking over my shoulder with every word that I write, you are such a part of it." "I do, too," she answered. This is a recipe, among many, for which she is famous.

RUM-PLUM JAM

4 cups prepared fruit	7½ cups sugar
¼ cup water	½ bottle liquid pectin
½ cup lemon juice	¼ cup rum

Pit, but do not peel plums, cut in small pieces and place in large saucepan. Crush, add water and bring to a boil.

Cover and simmer until soft, stirring frequently. Add lemon juice and sugar. Bring to boil, stirring constantly. Boil hard for one minute. Remove from heat, add ½ bottle liquid pectin and stir; add rum and stir. Pour into scalded glasses, top jam with a thin layer of melted paraffin. When jam is cool, place covers on top.

MAINE BLUEBERRY JAM

6 cups blueberries
1 box powdered pectin
  (1 and ¾ ounces)

2 tablespoons lemon juice
4 cups sugar
Water, if needed

Crush ripe blueberries. Measure 4 cups berries and place in large saucepan. (Add water to make 4 cups, if needed). Add lemon juice and pectin to berries. Mix. Bring mixture to hard boil over high heat, stirring constantly. Add sugar all at once. Bring to rolling boil. Boil hard for one minute, again stirring constantly.

Remove from heat; skim off foam with metal spoon. Stir and skim alternately for 5 minutes to cool slightly and prevent fruits from floating. Ladle into scalded jelly glasses. Cover with thin layer melted paraffin. This will yield eight 6-ounce glasses.

GRAPE CONSERVE

About 4 pounds
  Concord grapes
1 orange
4 cups sugar

1 cup seedless raisins
1 cup chopped walnuts
½ teaspoon salt

Separate and wash grapes, remove skins — do not discard skins. Place pulp minus skins in saucepan. Bring to boiling point and boil 10 minutes. Stir frequently. Press through sieve to remove seeds.

Put orange, skin and all through coarse blade of food chopper, catching any juice that you can.

Add to grape pulp the ground orange with juice, sugar, raisins and salt. Boil rapidly, stirring constantly, until mixture thickens or about 10 minutes. Add grape skins. Boil 10 minutes longer. Remove from heat.

Add walnuts, mix well. Pour into hot clean jars and seal.

★Red pepper jam is a very special treat and so easy to make. A recipe came to me from Bar Harbor when, once upon a time, Maine cooks submitted favorite recipes for a national food preservation contest. I cannot recall if this recipe won an award, but it should have.

RED PEPPER JAM

15 large sweet red peppers   1 tablespoon salt

Grind the peppers fine in meat grinder. Add salt and allow to stand overnight. In morning drain well. Add:

3 cups sugar   2 cups vinegar

Boil for 20 minutes, taking care not to burn. Do not strain. Put in scalded jelly glasses. Cover with melted paraffin. When jam is cold, place tops on jars.

★And then there's tomato flip-flap, another entry in this contest from an Augusta friend.

TOMATO FLIP-FLAP

7 pounds ripe tomatoes,   3 pounds sugar
   peeled and sliced   1 tablespoon whole cloves
Vinegar

Cover tomatoes with vinegar and allow to stand overnight. In morning drain, discard the vinegar. Add sugar and whole cloves, mixing the cloves right into the tomato mixture. Bring to a quick boil, then cook over low heat until it jells. Turn into sterilized jelly glasses and seal with melted paraffin. This relish is especially nice with roast beef, but is good with any meat.

★Candied dills may be made just any time of year, because you will only need to buy a quart of whole dill pickles. From then on it is an easy matter to make them into this delicious pickle:

CANDIED DILLS

1 quart whole dill pickles   ¼ cup vinegar
   (not Kosher)   1 teaspoon celery seed
1½ cups sugar   1 teaspoon mustard seed

Drain pickles and discard juice. Slice into a mixing bowl. Add sugar, vinegar, celery seed and mustard seed. Stir periodically for 3 to 4 hours, then bottle in the original jar. Use smaller jars if you want to use them for gifts.

★In making pickles, here are a few suggestions we need to give thought to, for best results:

1. Avoid using iodized salt in pickles. Buy coarse salt. This was formerly referred to as "bag" salt; it now comes in boxes and is especially recommended for pickle-making. It is preferable to table salt for no cornstarch is added, resulting in pickles that are not cloudy.

2. A brine is a solution of salt and water; usually one part coarse salt to nine parts water.

3. Read the label on the vinegar you buy; a 5% vinegar is best for pickling.

4. Soaking pickles overnight? Use pottery or enamel pan or stainless steel kettle for this, as well as in cooking the pickles.

5. Store pickles in well-sealed crocks or preferably in jars with glass tops, to avoid corrosion.

TASTY PICKLES

Pack washed and dried small cucumbers into sterilized quart jar. Add 2 tablespoons dry mustard, 2 tablespoons salt and 2 tablespoons sugar to jar. Fill jar with vinegar. Cover securely and shake jar so ingredients are well mixed. Shake occasionally. The pickles are ready for eating in about two weeks.

Can you think of an easier way to make a quart of old-fashioned sour pickles? Especially if you have just about enough small cucumbers to fill a quart jar.

★This delightful pickle recipe only came my way recently. "Em" came to visit Maine friends and that is how I met her. When she returned to her own big farm in Nebraska, she sent this pickle recipe. She pleased all Maine people when she shared this recipe with us. It is an uncooked pickle and is really kept refrigerated.

REFRIGERATED CUCUMBER PICKLES

25 not too large cucumbers	5 cups sugar
3 onions, medium size	1 teaspoon turmeric
½ cup pickling salt	1½ teaspoons celery seed
4 cups cider vinegar	1½ teaspoons mustard seed

Wash and wipe cucumbers. Peel onions. Slice unpared cucumbers and peeled onions as for table use, making these thin slices. Mix all other ingredients and pour over slices. Mix together lightly. Place in glass jars for storage, cover jars and keep refrigerated. Delicious!

★This is another Down East recipe from the Calais area — and it is named icicle pickles. Don't let the name fool you, although ice cubes are part of the recipe. In this recipe the syrup mixture is heated.

ICICLE PICKLES

Cut cucumbers lengthwise, leaving the parings on. Place in a large bowl, cover with cold water and ice cubes for 3 hours, adding more ice as it melts. Drain thoroughly and pack cucumbers into quart jars, standing the cucumbers upright. Insert a few onion slices and a stalk of celery, then fill jars with pickling syrup made as follows:

1 quart cider vinegar	1 tablespoon mustard seed
1½ cups sugar	1 tablespoon celery seed
½ cup salt	

Bring this mixture to boiling point and pour into jars. Seal tight; do not use for 2 months.

★Maybe you call it piccalilli but my mother always called it Indian relish. There was always a crock of it down cellar at the farm and we liked it best with baked beans.

INDIAN RELISH

1 peck green tomatoes   1 cup salt

Chop green tomatoes, sprinkle with salt. Let set overnight. Drain. Then add:

1 medium cabbage,   3 quarts vinegar
   chopped fine

Boil slowly for 30 minutes. Then add:

6 onions, chopped   8 cups sugar
3 hot red peppers, chopped   2 tablespoons celery seed
2 sweet green peppers,   2 tablespoons mustard seed
   chopped

Mix this together. Then make a small cheesecloth bag, put one tablespoon stick cinnamon and one tablespoon whole cloves into bag and tie securely, then place in pickle mixture. Cook all together until vegetables are soft. Ladle into sterilized jars and seal immediately.

BREAD AND BUTTER
PICKLES

4 quarts unpared cucumber   4 small onions, peeled
   slices cut about ⅛ inch   and sliced thin
   thick, using cucumbers
   that are not too large

Place these slices in an earthenware bowl; mix 4 cups cold water with ½ cup pickling salt and pour over slices. Let stand overnight.

In the morning drain and mix with following ingredients that have been brought to boiling point:

3 cups sugar   1 tablespoon mustard seed
3 cups vinegar   1 tablespoon celery seed

Use large enough kettle to bring these to boiling point, then add drained cucumber and onion slices. Bring back to boil, cook until cucumber slices are tender, slightly less than 15 minutes. Have hot sterilized jars ready, ladle mixture into them. Seal. Makes about 5 pints.

APPLE AND GREEN TOMATO RELISH

12 medium sized apples,
　pared and cored
8 medium sized green
　tomatoes
4 onions, peeled
3½ cups sugar
1½ cups vinegar

1 tablespoon salt
1 tablespoon mixed spices
　in a bag (net is good
　for this)
2 sweet green peppers
1 hot red pepper

Grind apples, green tomatoes, onions and seeded peppers. Parings may be left on apples if you wish. Combine all ingredients in kettle and cook until mixture is transparent. Remove bag of spices and ladle into sterilized jars and seal. If the hot pepper is too large, use only half.

★Since this pickle recipe has turmeric in it, I have to tell you a little story. For the longest while after I started writing my column, if a pickle recipe had this ingredient, I spelled it just as it sounded — tumeric. It didn't get picked up and that is the way it was used until there came a day when I guess a reader could stand it no longer. She wrote me a letter and stated, "Mrs. Standish, will you please spell turmeric correctly." No name was signed and I did appreciate having her tell me this, although the big dictionary does list tumeric as a variant.

SLICED ZUCCHINI PICKLES

1 quart vinegar
2 cups sugar
½ cup salt
2 teaspoons celery seed

2 teaspoons turmeric
1 teaspoon dry mustard
4 quarts sliced, unpared
　zucchini squash
1 quart onions, sliced

Bring vinegar, sugar, salt and spices to a boil. Pour this hot mixture over small zucchini squash sliced thin and thinly sliced onion slices. Let stand one hour. Bring to a boil, cook 3 minutes. Pack in hot sterilized jars, seal at once. Makes 6 pints.

★I had quite forgotten about this recipe for dilled string beans and when someone commented on my good recipe for doing these, I remarked, "I agree, that recipe in Cooking Down East is delicious." She answered, "But Marge, that's not the one I use. It's one you had in your column another time."

DILLED STRING BEANS

2 quarts green or
  wax beans
4 small dry red peppers
  (from your package of
  pickling spice)
4 small cloves garlic,
  left whole

4 heads green dill
  (this means fresh)
2 cups vinegar
2 cups water
¼ cup salt

Cut ends off beans, leave whole. Wash beans and steam 20 minutes or boil for 10 minutes. Pack into sterilized pint jars. To each pint jar add 1 small red hot pepper, 1 clove garlic and 1 head fresh green dill.

Bring vinegar, water and salt to a boil. When boiling, turn into prepared pint jars. Seal. Makes 4 pints. Store 6 weeks before using. That's a long time but it's worth it. These make a delicious party food.

CORN RELISH

18 large ears corn,
  uncooked
4 large onions, chopped
2 sweet green peppers,
  seeded and chopped
1 sweet red pepper,
  seeded and chopped

1½ pounds light brown
  sugar
¼ cup pickling salt
3 tablespoons celery seed
3¼ tablespoons dry
  mustard
2 quarts vinegar

Cut corn from cob but do not scrape the ears, mix with onions and peppers, then add remaining ingredients. A lot depends upon the size of the kernels of corn — you may need the entire 2 quarts vinegar and you may not. Watch it, not to make it too soupy. Cook slowly for 20 to 30 minutes in enamel or stainless steel kettle, stirring occasionally and taking care that it does not burn. Ladle relish into sterilized jars and seal. This should make 5 pints.

KOSHER HALF-SOURS

12 small cucumbers	2 quarts water
¼ cup pickling salt	1 teaspoon whole
½ cup vinegar	pickling spice
	1 clove garlic

Put scrubbed cukes in agate or stoneware pan. In a saucepan combine salt, water and vinegar, bring to a boil. Boil two minutes. Pour over the cukes and cover with a flat plate, weighted down with a heavy stone (scrubbed, of course). Leave this on kitchen counter and when cool, put in a large jar such as a gallon or half-gallon jug, making sure brine covers cukes. Add spices, garlic, put in a bay leaf if you like, cover jar lightly with wax paper. Keep at room temperature for 3 days, then cover and keep refrigerated.

These half-sours must be kept refrigerated, for the proportion of vinegar to water is so small that they would spoil quickly if not refrigerated. You could do green tomato half-sours in this same way.

CUCUMBER PICKLES

Soak 1 peck of not-too-large cucumbers in a weak brine overnight. Mix brine by using ½ cup pickling salt to 1 quart water. Mix enough to cover the peck of cucumbers that have been washed and wiped before covering with brine.

In morning drain cucumbers, returning cukes to kettle, then pour over them following liquid that has been heated to boiling point:

1 ½ quarts vinegar   1 cup sugar
1 ½ quarts water   ½ cup pickling salt

Let stand ½ hour after pouring hot liquid on cucumbers. Pack into hot, sterilized jars. Return liquor to heat and again bring to boiling point. Pour over tightly packed cukes in jars. Add 1 teaspoon whole pickling spice to each quart pickles. Seal.

POTSFIELD PICKLE

Cut into small pieces and measure:

6 cups peeled,   2 onions, chopped
  ripe tomatoes   2 green peppers, chopped
6 cups unpeeled
  green tomatoes

Add ¼ cup pickling salt and let this mixture stand overnight. In the morning drain for 1 hour. Place drained vegetables in a large kettle and add:

2 cups sugar   1 teaspoon powdered cloves
1 pint vinegar   1 teaspoon cinnamon

Cook until soft. Turn into hot sterilized jars and seal.

EASY MINCEMEAT

3 pounds hamburg or about   1 ½ cups seedless raisins
  6 cups, uncooked   1 ½ cups diced
12 cups apples, chopped,   candied fruit
  and cored but with par-   3 teaspoons cinnamon
  ings left on   3 teaspoons powdered
3 cups sugar   cloves
3 cups molasses   2 teaspoons nutmeg
2 cups cider or 1   1 tablespoon salt
  cup vinegar

Combine all ingredients and cook on low heat for several hours until apples are soft and all the ingredients are well blended. Turn into sterilized jars, or into freezer container if you prefer freezing the mincemeat. Makes 6 pint jars.

★The neighbors across the street freeze unlimited produce from their garden. I would have to say their specialty is freezing cut corn and I enjoy watching the entire procedure. This is a combined effort and it goes like this:

FREEZING CUT CORN

The quicker the trip from garden to freezer, no matter what you are freezing, the better the results. This bears out the thought that the results are only as good as what you start with, so use fresh produce.

While husking the fresh corn, have a kettle of water coming to the boiling point, for blanching. Place husked corn in boiling water, cover kettle, bring to a boil and time this for four minutes.

Using tongs, place corn in a colander, set in a large kettle under the cold water faucet, let cold water run over the corn until it is cold.

If you have a corn cutter, use it for removing corn from cob. If not, use a flat kitchen knife called a case knife. Cut off corn and use back of knife for scraping remainder of corn from cob. Fill freezer packages with the cut corn, seal, label package and into the freezer it goes. Actually, a simple procedure. It is wise not to attempt too much at one time.

FREEZING FRESH BLUEBERRIES

Dry Pack: Place picked-over blueberries in freezer containers, without washing. They can wait to be washed when they are used. Seal berries and put into freezer. You will find the plastic containers with tight covers excellent for freezing berries and other foods. Frankly, I add the frozen berries just as they come from the freezer to batters or put them into pies in their frozen state. Try blueberry muffins for breakfast some Sunday morning next January, just to remind you of the fun you had last summer.

★A blueberry pie made and frozen, to be baked later on, gives a comfortable feeling to any housewife. It happens

I like to do it this way, although many cooks prefer to bake a berry or fruit pie, cool it, then wrap securely using foil. That is up to the cook. These same suggestions work for any fruit or berry pie.

FREEZING BLUEBERRY PIE

Prepare a blueberry pie as if you were going to bake it right then, except do not cut vents in the top crust. Wrap securely in foil, carefully seal, place in freezer. When you decide to bake the pie, remove from freezer, cut vents (not more than three small ones), place frozen pie in oven. Bake at same temperature as you would any fruit or berry pie, in this case at 425 degrees for 40 minutes. Then, because it is baked from its frozen state, add 15 minutes. Do this for all unbaked frozen pies. Do not be a bit concerned about using a glass pie plate. It will not crack nor break as long as it is not wet on the outside, so always get a frozen pie right from the freezer into the hot oven.

★I've tried freezing thick slices of ripe tomatoes but I like the feeling of canning ripe tomatoes. It is an easy procedure, using a boiling water bath, and they may be canned in pints or quarts.

CANNING RIPE TOMATOES

Use only sound tomatoes. Let stand in boiling water for about a minute or until skins are loosened, dip in cold water, cut out stems and remove skins. These may be canned whole or cut into quarters, which is what I prefer doing. It is not easy to find canned stewed tomatoes in the markets now.

Heat in a large saucepan to the boiling point. Pack into pint or quart jars. I use pint jars because the kettle I use for the boiling water bath is the right size to hold 4 pints.

The jars must have been sterilized, the covers too. They must be kept hot. Place ½ teaspoon salt into bottoms of pint jars, 1 teaspoon salt in quart jars. Place fresh jar rubber on, then fill with hot tomatoes, make certain mouth of jar is clean, place cover on jar, partially seal. Place immediately in boiling water bath, make certain water covers tops of jars by one inch. Place cover back on canning kettle. Bring immediately to a boil. Boil for 10 minutes, either pints or quarts.

Remove jars carefully, place on rack to cool. Adjust covers immediately to complete seal, so they are all clamped or screwed on completely. Allow jars to cool right side up and out of drafts. Store in cool, dark, dry place.

★Can you freeze mushrooms is a question often asked. Here is a good method. A month is about as long as you would want to keep mushrooms frozen. Which brings up a remark handed on to me and which I like to repeat. Remember that the food you put into a freezer is in a "checking account, not a savings account."

TO FREEZE FRESH MUSHROOMS

Select top grade unopened fresh mushrooms. Place in rigid containers and seal tops. Freeze. Do not clean or prepare at all. When ready to use, cut off the tips of the stems and wipe. Mushrooms should not be washed. And they are never peeled. A damp paper towel will be good for cleaning mushrooms.

FREEZING ASPARAGUS

Break off the lower part of the stalk where it snaps easily. Wash and trim off lower scales. Cut stalks to fit box and stand them in blanching basket. Have boiling water about one inch deep in kettle. Drop in basket, cover, and time 2 to 4 minutes. Remove basket and plunge into ice water, moving it so it cools rapidly. Drain on absorbent towels and pack into top opening box. Seal and place in freezer.

TO FREEZE SQUASH

Prepare as for table with or without salting. Cool thoroughly, package and freeze.

These "Firsts" Came Last, Too

*Mankind is divisible
into two great classes:
Hosts and Guests*

CHAPTER ELEVEN

These "Firsts" Came Last, Too

This is where you will find the party food. I have a strong feeling that in a Maine cookbook the first chapter should be on the kind of food for which we are famous. That is why soups, stews and chowders are in the first chapter of this book, as they were in Cooking Down East.

Unlike many cookbooks where you find the first chapter on appetizers and the like, these "firsts" came in the last chapter and that of course, is the reason for its name.

These recipes have all come from Maine cooks, who delight in sharing their ideas for party food. There is one to fit almost every occasion. You will find hors d'oeuvre suggestions of all kinds, both hot and cold. There are recipes for sandwich fillings and other party foods.

It is a well-known fact that the food that greets the guests makes the first impression. However, if you are serving a delicious dinner to your guests, it is well to remember that appetizers should serve to whet, rather than dull, the appetite. It is wise to keep the "firsts" you serve with drinks long on quality and short on quantity.

These recipes have all appeared in my column. I hope the choice I have made for this last chapter will be just what you have been looking for.

★Here is a dip that is certain to be popular with the men when you entertain. It is unusual to find cooked chicken in a dip. The addition of chopped cashew nuts just before serving will give it a delightful flavor. Why don't you let your guests decide what is in this dip. They'll wonder.

CURRIED CHICKEN DIP

Combine in blender until smooth:

One 5-ounce jar boned
  chicken or 1 cup cooked
  chicken
One 3-ounce can
  mushrooms, drained

1 cup commercial
  sour cream
2 to 3 teaspoons
  curry powder

Chill. Just before serving add ½ cup chopped cashew nuts. This is good served with crispy raw vegetables or crackers or chips.

DEVILED HAM DIP

Two 4½-ounce cans
  deviled ham
One 8-ounce package
  cream cheese
2 tablespoons chopped
  stuffed olives

1 tablespoon catsup
1 to 2 teaspoons finely
  minced onion

Combine ingredients and chill. Garnish with extra chopped olives. Serve with crackers.

BOLOGNA ROLL-UPS

Spread slices of bologna with softened cream cheese mixed with chives that have been snipped, or horseradish. Roll up, fasten with toothpicks. Chill. Slice into bite-size pieces and serve.

EASY SPREAD

Peanut butter   Sweet onion relish

Use these two ingredients half and half. Mix and pile into a small serving bowl. Place in center of serving plate. Surround with crackers of your choice, provide with a knife for spreading, and you are ready with a delicious party spread. If you prefer a dip, add more sweet onion relish. You will find jars of this relish in your market.

AVOCADO DIP

1 large, fully ripe avocado	¼ cup finely minced onion
One 8-ounce package	1 teaspoon salt
cream cheese	Worcestershire sauce,
3 tablespoons lemon juice	to taste

Blend cream cheese and avocado until smooth. Add remaining ingredients and mix well. Serve in a bowl with crisp crackers. Corn chips are especially good with avocado dip.

If you decide to use only the avocado, cut down on the seasonings. The lemon juice keeps the avocado from turning dark. This freezes well. Cream cheese is used in this dip to extend the avocado.

A true Guacamole, which of course is the right name for an avocado dip, would not use cream cheese. A fresh tomato, skinned and chopped, would be added, as well as 1 tablespoon chopped green chili peppers to 2 avocados, and 1 teaspoon chopped fresh coriander leaves not available in our Maine markets. Trouble pronouncing Guacamole? Say wah-kah-moh-leh. Not a bit Maine-ish but a delicious dip and very popular.

MINI-PIZZAS

Ritz cheese crackers	Thin pieces sharp cheese
Very thin dill pickle slices	Oregano

These mini-pizzas can be prepared an hour ahead, then broiled. You will find the jars of very thin pickles in your market, called hamburger dill slices. Lay these on a paper towel to drain. Place cheese crackers on a cookie sheet. Lay a drained pickle slice on each, top with a thin slice of sharp cheese. Sprinkle with a shake of oregano. Place pan under broiler, with oven door open as in all broiling. Watch carefully, allow to broil 3 to 5 minutes. Serve while hot.

SESAME ROUNDS

Lay a thin piece of sharp cheese on round sesame crackers, sprinkle top of cheese with onion salt. Place pan under broiler and watch carefully. Serve when cheese melts.

TRISCUIT SQUARES

Triscuits	Orange marmalade
Peanut butter	Bacon

Spread triscuit crackers with peanut butter, put a dab of orange marmalade in center, top with a small piece of raw bacon. Place these on a cookie sheet, place under broiler. Broil only until the bacon cooks and dribbles down into the orange marmalade and peanut butter.

★Serving roasted potato strips is a good way of showing off Maine potatoes. These are especially good and so inexpensive. They will become a standard appetizer at your parties.

ROASTED POTATO STRIPS

5 or 6 Maine baking potatoes	Salt and pepper
Margarine at room temperature	

Bake potatoes at 450 degrees for 50 minutes or until done. Place baked potato on wooden board, cut in half the long way. Scoop out the baked potato and use as whipped potato.

Spread softened margarine on inside and outside of baked potato skin, cut it into long strips just under ½-inch wide. Use the inside of a fresh looking brown paper bag, cut to fit on a cookie sheet.

Lay the strips skin-side up on the brown paper. Sprinkle with salt and pepper. Only one side needs seasoning. Bake at 400 degrees about 8 minutes. They do not need turning, as the inside of strips get golden brown as they bake. Cool on brown paper. These will be crisp and delicious.

ONION-FLAVORED WALNUTS

½ pound (2 cups) walnut halves or pieces	3 tablespoons dry onion soup mix
2 tablespoons butter or margarine	

Spread nuts on baking sheet and dot with butter. Bake in 350-degree oven for 15 to 20 minutes. Stir often. Remove from oven and sprinkle with dry onion soup mix, tossing lightly. Cool on paper towels.

★Tiny meat balls served hot disappear fast at parties. This recipe from Winthrop friends is especially good. You will like to prepare these because, like many recipes of this kind, they may be done ahead. You will enjoy "spearing" these with toothpicks, too.

APPETIZER MEAT BALLS

¾ pound ground lean beef
¼ pound ground lean pork
¾ cup uncooked rolled oats
½ cup milk
¼ cup finely chopped water
   chestnuts, or walnuts
   may be substituted

1 tablespoon
   Worcestershire sauce
½ teaspoon salt
½ teaspoon garlic salt
2 tablespoons margarine
Dash of Tabasco sauce

Mix all ingredients except margarine. Shape into four dozen small balls. Brown well in the margarine. Place on paper toweling to drain. Add to sweet-sour sauce that has been prepared, and simmer for 30 minutes. Serve hot, using toothpicks for spearing.

SWEET-SOUR SAUCE

Mix together in a large skillet, not aluminum:

1 cup sugar
¾ cup vinegar
¾ cup water

1 teaspoon paprika
½ teaspoon salt

Heat 5 minutes, blend 2 tablespoons cornstarch with 1 tablespoon water. Stir into hot mixture and continue to stir until sauce is thickened.

★Miniature drumsticks are a popular finger food at parties. Use the "drumstick" half of the wing for these, which of course look exactly like small drumsticks.

MINIATURE DRUMSTICKS

3 pounds broiler-fryer
  chicken wings (about 18)
1½ cups toasted bread
  crumbs or ¾ cup flour
½ cup freshly grated
  Parmesan cheese

1 teaspoon salt
¼ teaspoon pepper
½ teaspoon Ac'cent
1 stick margarine, melted

Discard tips from wings; disjoint wings or cut in half and use the "drumstick" half only for this recipe. Blend crumbs or flour, cheese, salt, pepper and Ac'cent.

Wash and wipe "drumsticks." Dip each piece in melted margarine, then in crumb mixture. Place on a shallow pan, like a jelly roll pan. You may want to line pan with foil, then lay "drumsticks" on it. Bake at 350 degrees for 35 to 40 minutes or until they are fork-tender. Serve hot.

★Hot bacon-wrapped appetizers have great appeal, and whether you use oysters, chicken livers or water chestnuts, they are all good. Probably the name of the first one makes it most popular.

ANGELS ON HORSEBACK

24 plump raw oysters
¼ cup lemon juice
3 dashes Tabasco sauce

1 teaspoon Worcestershire
½ teaspoon salt
12 strips bacon

Drain oysters on paper toweling. Place in bowl, add lemon juice, Tabasco, Worcestershire and salt. Stir to coat oysters with sauce. Cut each bacon strip in half, use each half to wrap an oyster. Secure with toothpicks. Place on a rack in baking dish. Bake at 450 degrees until bacon is crisp.

CHICKEN LIVER
WRAP-UPS

Cook chicken livers in a small amount of boiling salted water about 15 minutes, or until tender. Drain. Wrap each cooked chicken liver in a ½ slice bacon, cut crosswise.

Fasten bacon in place with toothpicks. Place wrap-ups on a rack in baking pan. Bake at 425 degrees until bacon is crisp. Serve hot with toothpicks still in place.

SWEET-SOUR WATER CHESTNUTS

One 6-ounce can water chestnuts (about 24 pieces)
½ cup vinegar
½ cup liquid from chestnuts
12 bacon strips, cut in half
Brown sugar

Marinate chestnut pieces for 1 hour in vinegar and chestnut liquid. Drain. Spread each half slice of bacon with brown sugar. Roll chestnuts in bacon slices and fasten with toothpicks. Place in a shallow pan. Bake at 350 degrees for 30 minutes. Serve hot. These have a Far Eastern flavor — not Down Eastern.

FRANKFORTS-RANGELEY STYLE

One 9-ounce can pineapple tidbits, not drained
One 8-ounce can seasoned tomato sauce
1 tablespoon brown sugar
1 tablespoon vinegar
1 tablespoon prepared mustard
1 tablespoon finely chopped onion
½ to 1 teaspoon chili powder
½ teaspoon salt
1 pound frankforts, cut in bite-size pieces

Simmer all together in saucepan for ½ to 1 hour. Serve hot, using toothpicks for spearing.

★Come now, you're not afraid of a tiny cream puff, are you? Filled with whatever your choice might be, they make delicious party food. Best of all, they may be made weeks ahead for, once they are baked and cooled, they may be placed in a plastic bag, sealed and put in the freezer. Come party time they are thawed, then filled with your choice, depending upon the kind of party you are having.

TINY CREAM PUFFS

1 cup water	1 cup sifted flour
1 stick margarine	4 eggs

Put water into a saucepan and bring to a boil, add stick of margarine and allow it to melt. Quickly stir in the one cup sifted flour, using a wooden spoon. Turn the heat off as you do this, continuing to stir, and as soon as the mixture forms a ball in the center of the saucepan, remove from heat.

It is wisest if you break each egg into a cup, then turn it into the batter; no chance of getting a piece of shell in the batter. Add each egg one at a time, beating well after each addition. If you stir hard after adding each egg, the batter should keep stiff, which is the way it should be.

Use ungreased cookie sheets. You will get about 90 tiny cream puffs, so use about 1/2 teaspoon of mixture for each puff. As soon as one pan is ready, place on lower rack in a 400-degree oven. Bake for 15 minutes while preparing second pan.

At end of 15 minutes, place first pan on upper rack in oven and place second pan on lower rack. Probably that first pan will only need 10 minutes on the upper rack. Remove when tiny puffs are delicately baked. At end of 15 minutes, place the second pan on upper rack for about 10 minutes.

Place cream puffs on rack to cool. They may then be frozen or used in a short time. Using a paring knife, slit an opening and fill with chicken salad, ham salad or a fish salad. If you want to use them for a "sweet," fill with coffee-flavored whipped cream.

★This recipe for chicken liver puffs has a cream puff base. You have just learned that making cream puffs is a simple procedure, so now you can make these delicious appetizers. If you want to, try making them a bit larger than the recipe suggests and serve them for a light supper accompanied by a tossed salad and fruit. They will be good to serve for a morning coffee, but they are especially good made small and served at a cocktail party.

CHICKEN LIVER PUFFS

Sprinkle eight ounces of chicken livers with monosodium glutamate (Ac'cent) and brown in fry pan in 1 tablespoon oil until thoroughly cooked. Cool livers, remove membrane and chop very fine. Set aside. Prepare puff mixture as follows:

1 cup water	1 cup sifted flour
1 stick margarine	4 eggs

Bring water to a boil in a saucepan. Add stick of margarine and allow to melt. With a wooden spoon stir in all the flour at once. Turn off heat when you add flour. Continue stirring mixture vigorously until mixture leaves sides and forms a ball in center of pan.

Remove from stove and, while mixture is still hot, add eggs one at a time, beating hard after each addition. The mixture should be stiff and smooth.

Add dry onion soup mix to puff batter. The recipe says one envelope of the mix. I prefer about two tablespoons for seasoning. Fold in the chopped livers. Mix well and drop by half teaspoonfuls onto ungreased cookie sheets. Use teaspoonfuls if you want larger puffs.

Bake at 400 degrees for about 30 minutes. You will need two cookie sheets. Change pans in oven, top for bottom, after about 20 minutes of baking.

These may be baked. cooled, frozen, then reheated for serving. Just make certain they are served piping hot from the oven.

HOT DOG ROLL-UPS

A tube of refrigerated crescent rolls	A can of Vienna sausage may be substituted for
A package of the small cocktail hot dogs	the cocktail franks
	Hot dog mustard

Unwrap the dough triangles, cut each in half the long way, spread lightly with hot dog mustard and roll up a piglet in each. No toothpicks are needed. Place on cookie sheet and bake for 10 minutes at 375. Serve hot.

★Ways of making sandwiches are always in demand for home, picnic or otherwise. Here are a number of favorites.

CHOPPED HOT DOG FILLING

Place left-over cooked hot dogs in a wooden bowl. Using à chopping knife, chop quite fine. Add black pepper and mayonnaise. Mix and use as sandwich filling. It is delicious.

CUCUMBER OPEN-FACED SANDWICHES

Using a 1½ or 2-inch biscuit cutter, cut rounds of bread from regular slices of bread. These are open face so a regular thickness works fine, although thinly-sliced bread is daintier for a tea. Spread these bread rounds with mayonnaise.

Pare cucumber. Using a dinner fork, draw the tines down the sides of the pared cucumber and slice it thin. Place a round on each prepared round of bread. Give a light dusting of paprika to the center of each cucumber slice. No mayonnaise is needed on top, since that on the bread round is enough.

These may be prepared ahead. Dampen a fresh linen dish towel and lay on a cookie sheet or tray. Cover with wax paper, place cucumber sandwiches on wax paper, cover lightly with plastic wrap, and keep in refrigerator.

★It's as simple as can be if you want thinly sliced bread for sandwiches. Using regular sliced bread, merely cut off the crusts and use a rolling pin to roll the slices to the thinness you like.

CHEESE PIMIENTO SANDWICH FILLING

½ pound American cheese   2 tablespoons pimiento,
A bit of onion juice   minced
                                                      Mayonnaise to mix

Put cheese through food grinder. Dice pimiento into tiny bits. Scrape a bit of onion juice into mixture, add enough mayonnaise to mix. Store in refrigerator until time to use.

DRIED-BEEF SANDWICH

Open a jar of dried beef. Lay thin slices on slice of buttered bread. Spread with mayonnaise. No other seasoning needed. Top with slice of bread. This is hearty and simple to make.

★If you are entertaining at a morning coffee, this recipe is delicious with hot coffee.

ORANGE MARMALADE
ROLL-UPS

Using loaf of regular sliced bread, place slices on board, cut off crusts. With rolling pin roll each slice thin. Spread with orange marmalade. Roll up and secure with 2 toothpicks. Spread softened margarine on top of each. Place in foil-lined pan. Bake at 400 degrees for 15 minutes or until toasty-brown. Remove toothpicks and serve hot.

★This is a sweet filling and is good for a tea sandwich. It tastes best as a filling for white bread.

TUTTI-FRUITTI
SANDWICH FILLING

1 pound dates	1 ¼ cups walnuts
6 ounces figs	About 1 ½ cups orange
1 ½ cups seedless raisins	juice

Grind fruits and nuts together, moisten with orange juice. Use 2 tablespoons of filling per sandwich, using white bread.

★Mint cooler is a Gardiner favorite and is often used in the summer months at teas.

MINT COOLER

2 cups sugar
4 heaping tablespoons tea, preferably black

4 lemons, juice and rind
8 sprigs fresh mint, about 6 inches long
1 gallon boiling water

Halve the lemons and squeeze out juice. Combine both juice and rinds in large kettle with other ingredients. Add 1 gallon of boiling water. Stir to dissolve sugar. Allow this to steep about 5 minutes — do this off the heat. Stir again and strain through a fresh cloth. Cool. This is important — add ice cubes just before serving.

PERCOLATOR PUNCH

1 tablespoon whole cloves
1½ teaspoons whole allspice
Three 2-inch pieces broken cinnamon sticks

¼ teaspoon salt
½ cup light brown sugar
3 cups water
3 cups pineapple juice

Place pineapple juice and water in a 9-cup percolator. Place remaining ingredients in the percolator basket. Perk for 10 minutes. Remove the basket and serve hot. Serves 8 to 10.

MY FAVORITE FRUIT CUP

One 1-pound can grapefruit sections

Juice squeezed from 3 oranges
Sugar, to taste

Drain grapefruit sections, reserve juice for a mid-morning snack. Cut sections into bite-size pieces, place in a bowl. Turn freshly squeezed orange juice into grapefruit. Add sugar to taste, stir to dissolve. Cover and place in refrigerator to mellow. May be made several days ahead. Serve in sherbet glasses, topped with a cherry or a fresh strawberry.

By The Way - You Asked For More

When you have written a cookbook, you learn that there's an important part of the book to almost every homemaker. Over and over, when people learned this cookbook was underway, they cautioned, "You won't forget cooking hints and suggestions, will you?"

You asked for more so, to remind you when a question pops into your mind, here are your helpful hints:

WEIGHTS AND MEASURES

1 teaspoon   = 1/3 tablespoon
2 tablespoons   = 1 ounce
4 tablespoons   = ¼ cup
5 1/3 tablespoons = 1/3 cup
8 tablespoons   = ½ cup
1 cup   = ½ pint
2 cups   = 1 pint (1 pound)
2 pints   = 1 quart (2 pounds)
4 quarts   = 1 gallon (8 pounds)
16 ounces   = 1 pound
16 fluid ounces   = 1 pint (2 cups)
2 cups granulated sugar = 1 pound
2¼ cups firmly packed brown sugar = 1 pound
3½ cups confectioners sugar = 1 pound
1 tablespoon butter = ½ ounce
1 stick butter = ½ cup
½ pound butter = 1 cup
1 square unsweetened chocolate = 1 ounce
1 pound cheddar cheese makes about 4 cups shredded
1 cup raw rice will produce 3 cups cooked rice
1 cup macaroni makes 2 cups when cooked
1 cup dry beans makes 3 cups when cooked
1 slice bread makes ½ cup crumbs
18 to 20 small crackers make 1 cup crumbs
6 graham crackers make 1 cup crumbs

SUBSTITUTIONS

INSTEAD OF THIS:	USE:
1 teaspoon baking powder	¼ teaspoon soda + ½ teaspoon cream of tartar
1 square chocolate	3 tablespoons cocoa + 1 tablespoon shortening
1 tablespoon cornstarch	2 tablespoons flour
¾ cup cracker crumbs	1 cup dry bread crumbs
1 cup sour milk	1 cup sweet milk + 1 to 2 tablespoons vinegar or lemon juice
1 egg	2 egg yolks + 1 tablespoon water
In place of chocolate bits	"Jimmies"

HAVE YOU EVER?

Added dry potato flakes to any of the milk chowders for added flavor.

Added grated orange peel to your date recipes.

Grated the rind of an orange you are eating or squeezing, wrapped it in plastic and stored it in your freezer for future use.

Pan broiled your steak or hamburg by using a layer of salt in the pan instead of grease.

You won't forget, will you, to measure liquid in a glass measuring cup at eye level. The 1-cup line is below the rim of the cup to allow for accurate measuring.

For dry ingredients, the one-cup measure at the rim is a must for accuracy.

The nest of four and even 6 measuring cups is most helpful of all, especially when a recipe calls for 1/3 or 2/3 of a cup.

Above all, you will not forget to keep cooking happily, will you, for that is The Maine Way.

INDEX